D0008360

COOK TO BANG

The Lay Cook's Guide to Getting Laid

SPENCER WALKER

ST. MARTIN'S GRIFFIN

NEW YORK

COOK TO BANG. Copyright © 2010 by Spencer Walker. All rights reserved. Printed in the United States of America. For information, address St. Martin's Press, 175 Fifth Avenue, New York, N.Y. 10010.

www.stmartins.com

All photographs by Noah Abrams

Book design by Level C

Library of Congress Cataloging-in-Publication Data

Walker, Spencer.
    Cook to bang : the lay cook's guide to getting laid / Spencer Walker.—1st ed.
        p.   cm.
    ISBN 978-0-312-60018-1
    1. Aphrodisiac cookery.   2. Seduction.   I. Title.
TX652.W22   2010
641.5'63—dc22

                                                                    2009046745

First Edition: May 2010

10   9   8   7   6   5   4   3   2   1

This book is dedicated to all the girls I loved before.

Contents

COOK TO BANG

1

Why Cook to Bang?

You may ask yourself, "Why *Cook to Bang*?"
I ask, "Why do anything else?"

The answer is basic survival. Humans must eat and procreate in order to perpetuate. If we do not, we will become the New Coke of evolution: a mistake doomed to extinction. Human history has proven that we are not just some cruel experiment performed by your respective deity. The reason? We effectively Cook and Bang.

Food and sex have been linked since the dawn of civilization. Cavemen once roasted saber-toothed tiger kebabs for their cave babes. This set the mood for Cro-Magnon copulation. Neanderthals knew the importance of cooking for their lovers. This has been lost on the modern dating population. Most of these First World suckers are willing to blow half their paycheck on a fancy dinner only to end up with a doggy bag and blue balls. Why?

Cooking to Bang doesn't require harvesting a kidney to pay for the dinner bill. You can avoid the awkward invitation inside after a date. And going the extra mile yields decadent dividends. Culinary skills are as essential to the art of seduction as a brush and easel are for painting. Be the Picasso in the pantry, Van Gogh up the grill, and shake your Monet maker. *Cook to Bang* offers simple, effective methods for enjoying the two greatest pleasures: food and sex.

Anyone can cook an amazing meal and bring out their date's inner slut. The only way for the human race to continue is to *eat* and *bang*. So do your part. Learn how to wine, dine, and sixty-nine your dream date with minimal harm to your credit card or self-esteem. *Cook to Bang* is based on three simple principles:

1. CHEAPER THAN A RESTAURANT
2. THEY'RE ALREADY IN YOUR HOME
3. YOU'RE DESSERT

CHEAPER THAN A RESTAURANT

This should be obvious to anyone who has taken a date to Chez Douchebag and part of their soul died when the check arrived. You put your financial stability on the line for a piece of strange. Perhaps you got laid six ways from Sunday. You may be walking bowlegged or threw your back out attempting some feat reserved for Cirque du Soleil. But I wager that you more likely ended up with a kiss on the cheek and, if you are lucky, the privilege to bankroll future platonic adventures. So just as an experiment, take a few steps back and imagine how the condition of your bank account and libido would fair cooking at home. Worst-case scenario: you would yield the same result for less cash. Do it right and you can skip the three-dates-before-banging rule. Regardless, it is the right move considering the current economy is more flaccid than a eunuch stuffing dollar bills in Rosie O'Donnell's G-string.

THEY'RE ALREADY IN YOUR HOME

The only thing more awkward than a first kiss is a prostate exam. (A doctor fingering a man's exit-only may feel odd, but at least there is a health benefit.) Your mental health will suffer should you be rejected or worse, not try at all. A word to the wise: it is better to regret something you have done than regret something you haven't. First kisses are nearly impossible to execute in the wrong setting: a restaurant, your date's parents' house, a purity ball. But your home is your private domain, your dungeon of decadence. The best part is there is no awkward invitation inside when you host a date in your pad. Asking them in after a regular date is a loaded question that puts your ego on the chopping block again. Why risk it? You can make your move in the privacy of your own comfort zone without Peeping Toms whacking it or prudish cops writing you a ticket for public indecency. You can be as indecent as your perverted mind can muster behind closed doors.

YOU'RE DESSERT

I imagine this should speak for itself. But for those who fail to grasp the concept of innuendo, pay attention. I'm using dessert to hint at sexual intercourse. That is when a man and woman, or two men, or two women (I'll get the popcorn), or any combination thereof lay together and share a grown-up hug. This usually comes at the end of the meal. After your date and you have finished your impressive meal, you move on to something sweet . . . your hot body covered in something sweeter. More on this later in chapter 12, Advanced CTB: Culinarylingus.

Simple, right? Just be your charming self, cook like a champ, and you will be banging. Your task is to find that special someone you plan to seduce. This book isn't a guide how to pick up that girl or boy of your dreams. There are plenty of books on the art of pickup. If you were clever enough to buy this book, you are clever enough to set up a simple dinner date. Perhaps it's an art chick you met at a gallery opening, a club slut at a techno dance party, or a redneck at a NASCAR rally. There is a key to unlock, or more accurately, unzip any door. Some of these doors bust wide open with nothing more than a compliment. Others take some finessing and caressing. Get their phone number and plan like a general in the final battle of a war. It is vital to understand your chosen conquest and how you can exploit them for your own perverted gains. I believe in you.

Curious how *Cook to Bang* came to exist? *Cook to Bang's* genesis came out of anthropological observations of the modern dating population. The clear pattern observed was poor execution of a tried-and-true plan: wine and dine. Simple enough, right? Apparently not. There is a clear disconnect for chumps who assume legs will open wider than a porn star's if they spend X amount of dollars on a meal. I have fielded countless phone calls from sexually frustrated friends heading home before 10 P.M. from dates they thought were slam-dunk sexcapades. They'll say, "I thought she was up for it. You'd think I'd at least get a hummer. That sushi dinner cost a hundred bucks!" Newsflash, suckers: there is no ratio for amount of money spent to sexual activity unless you hire a hooker. Chances are it would be cheaper and at least you would get your rocks off. The only problem is you risk incarceration, disease, and possibly ending up on next week's episode of *To Catch a Predator*.

So what's the solution? Cook to Bang, my friends. This is something I learned in college. I was a horny young man in my sexual prime without a cast-iron pot to piss in. What I needed was a hook to make me stand out from the frat-tastic douche-bags with their steroid enhanced muscles sporting Celtic knot tattoos and wearing backward baseball caps. I was a scrawny hippie with a weed habit that made Cheech and Chong look like lightweights. I also had a knack for thinking outside the box, which had landed me in detention in high school, but I knew was one of my true assets. I needed a cure stat for the blue balls I sported my entire first semester in college. Yes, you read that right. I did not bang or even kiss a girl my entire first semester of college. Pathetic, right? I agree. Instead of crying into my keg cup, I did something about it. The hook I found that made me stand out from the Chads, Daves, and Mikes of Eta Pi was to cook for the ladies.

The infancy of the Cook to Bang philosophy began in my dorm kitchen next to the laundry machines. Privacy was not an option back then for my little culinary study-break dates. But something unexpected and grand came about from my public ceremonies: my reputation for being a culinary wizard exploded. There weren't enough nights in a week to accommodate the demand for my services. I graduated from zero to hero by the end of my decadent second semester.

The only proper way to follow it up was to take Cook to Bang campus wide in my sophomore year. Enter the Culinary Arts Club cofounded by yours truly. We talked the school into bankrolling our events, and more important, our food. Our club hosted a multitude of events, including Rock and Sushi Roll parties and an epic pie bake-off with over two hundred pies entered. My partner in crime was a stunning girl with a knack for baking and a body that wouldn't quit. I would love to say that we banged like spider monkeys after every meeting, but I would be lying. I was the idea man, but she was organized and kept the club running smoothly. At the time I thought she was out of my league; forgive me, fellow cook-to-bangers. I was still a novice. But don't feel *too* bad for me—I bagged plenty of club members and event attendees. The ratio for our club was 10–1, girls to guys. I exploited the odds like Rain Man in Vegas.

This love for food evolved into me working as a chef at night and on weekends. I thought becoming a professional chef was an ideal career path. My dream, for a nanosecond, was to become the next Wolfgang Puck. That fantasy soon evaporated among the steam of the ten-thousandth dish I washed for six dollars an hour. The real rub was that I was always working during prime-time tail-chasing hours. So I preserved my love for cooking and quit. I am grateful for the knowledge I picked up working in a professional kitchen. Making tons of food for too many people without enough time prepares you for anything. Now cooking for dates is elementary, which frees up brainpower to focus on banging.

There was a time, dear reader, when I forgot about my own foolproof method. I escaped a toxic five-year relationship only to find that I had forgotten how to be single. Most of my twenties had been squandered and I was determined to savor the breadcrumbs of my youth. But like a chump, I reverted to the old date-at-restaurant-I-can't-afford routine. The only thing I scored was the bill, while my date ran off to a booty text. Amateur dating hour was getting tired. So when I picked up a wannabe actress at a Halloween party dressed like a slutty mime, I returned to my roots and invited her over for dinner. She was impressed with the orangasmic catfish that I learned to cook while on a vacation in the Mexican Riviera. This dish sent this girl's hands down my pants before I could serve the dessert. We banged all weekend, only stopping to eat.

Lying in bed, my fluids drained, my self-esteem soaring, cash still intact in my wallet, I coined the phrase "cook to bang." This simple, effective gospel had to be spread. Einstein had the theory of relativity, Newton the laws of physics, and I have Cook to Bang.

I started cooktobang.com to help my fellow man get nookie with deceptively simple recipes and methods. What began as a fun creative outlet, became its own monster. CTB readers vouched that this shit works:

"The perfect breakthrough for the 'Let's just be friends' talk."

"My girlfriend was so impressed she told her parents about it!"

"Thanks so much for your savory suggestions. Cook to Bang works for girls, too."

"It was the easiest time I'd ever had visiting down under."

"Adaptable to any orientation it seems, CTB is a gay man's culinary paradise."

I tapped into something vital, and I owed it to myself—to the world—to share the lessons I learned. The book you hold in your hands is the product of my labor—I hope it brings you as many laughs, gasps, and screaming orgasms as I have enjoyed.

During the course of the book, *Cook to Bang* will take you through the history of cooking and banging. You will learn how to determine and execute your culinary seduction goals. Planning a meal for maximum effect and minimal cost will become second nature. We will discuss various types in the dating pool and how to lure them into bed. You will know your shit when it comes to cooking with aphrodisiacs and what drinks pair best with them. *Cook to Bang* will arm you with tips for setting the mood, building chemistry, and transitioning from cooking to banging. Should your best-laid plans suffer from Murphy's Law, *Cook to Bang* has you covered. I hope you have an appetite, because *Cook to Bang* is about to satisfy all of your senses!

2

Cooking to Bang Through History

Human civilization and evolution would not be possible without cooking and banging. Procreation and the perpetuation of the human race are merely a side effect. Cooking has evolved from brontosaurus burgers to eight-course chef's tasting menus. Seduction started with clubbing your fancy then dragging them by the hair into your cave. It has now reached its pinnacle: Cook to Bang.

Culinary seduction no doubt began with Ugg, a smarter than average caveman with player instinct. This naughty Neanderthal saw a woolly mammoth get skewered by a lightning bolt and smelled the tantalizing scent of cooked meat. Ugg brought the meat back to the village and shared it with the hottest Cro-Magnon ladies and became the leader of the tribe. He was the alpha male who gave his people the fire that made inedible foods delectable. Ugg may not realize it, but his quest to get laid opened the world up for culinary innovation. His legacy is every civilization. None of them could exist without the knowledge of how to Cook to Bang. Not bad for a dude who didn't realize his opposable thumbs were good for anything other than spanking it.

3500BC   3100BC 2200BC 1600BC   1200BC 1100BC

MESOPOTAMIA 3500 BC–2340 BC

The Mesopotamians founded the first major human civilization in present-day Iraq. This was the original breadbasket of mankind with plenty of beer to wash down those carbs. Don't tell Dr. Atkins, but carbohydrates are the root of civilization. This fertile land made it easy to grow vegetables and grains; fish from the Tigris and Euphrates were plenty; and dates flavored just about everything. The Hanging Gardens of Babylon were not just a tribute to the well-hung king, but a homage to great food. They had many awesome fruits and vegetables we know and love today, like figs and apples. Beer was the drink of choice, and Mesopotamians rich and poor drank at banquets, festivals, and every morning. Talk about the breakfast of champions!

Mesopotamia was a hedonist's paradise. Everyone gave love to the main goddess Ishtar who presided over war, death, and sex. Banging was the Mesopotamian national pastime. The warriors would celebrate victories at Ishtar's temples with feasts that ended with them banging holy prostitutes. Every woman was required to sit in a temple and wait for the first man to throw money in her lap, and then bang the shit out of him. They could not leave until they spread their legs for the gods. Refusing was an unforgivable sin. Sex cults were the norm and they performed raunchy sex acts in public and beckoned the spectators to become participants. These misbehaving Mesopotamians

1000BC 509BC 500BC 300BC 1607AD 1799AD

gave birth to the first STDs, like the clap and syphilis. You're welcome!

Gilgamesh was a straight-up Babylonian badass. Legend says he was the son of a goddess. His paranoid grandfather, the king, threw him out of a high tower, but an eagle broke his fall. Gilgamesh grew up to be a superstar warrior who had his wicked way with half the Babylonian kingdom. But he had his sights set on the hard-bodied high priestess that only slept with the king. (For the record, CTB does not recommend banging Grandpa's mistresses.) Gilgamesh decided, "I guess I'll be king then." He took his grandfather out the old-fashioned way, by bitch-slapping him to death with his own crown. Gilgamesh then slaughtered a cow to honor Ishtar and grilled up some kebabs to share with the high priestess. He went on to become a great king famed for his strength, building a wall for his people when he wasn't feasting and fucking. All hail Gilgamesh!

ANCIENT EGYPT 3100 BC–30 BC

The people of the Nile enjoyed food in quantities and varieties previously unknown. The river was the source of fish, irrigation, travel for trade, and skinny-dipping. The Egyptians mastered preserving food by salting, drying, and curing. This prosperity allowed Egyptians to innovate with food, crafts, and sexual positions. The nobles and wealthy class stuffed their fat faces with all manner of bread, pastries, wine, beer, and cheese. Feasts would last days, where men and women of leisure kicked it on cushioned chairs stuffing their faces while enjoying music, storytelling, acrobats, and strippers. Even the commoners, whose lives consisted of disease, pestilence, and building pyramids to gratify the pharaohs' egos, enjoyed plenty of beer and bread. They were too sauced to realize their lives sucked crocodile balls.

The ancient Egyptians, commoners and elite alike, were total pervs. They celebrated bestiality, transgenderism, incest, exhibitionism, and adultery. Egyptians were the first civilization to use contraception (with cow dung—for reals), develop circumcision to eke out more sexual pleasure, and formulate aphrodisiac and abortion potions. The Egyptian god Chaos wanked his fellow gods and the living world into creation. Egyptian women worshipped the phallus to honor the god Osiris, whose turdbucket brother Set hacked him to pieces before the goddess Isis put him back together with a bigger penis. A holy dildo! The original Girls Gone Wild would flash their genitals during the festival of the goddess Bastet. Egypt claims the original bachelorette parties: women sat in the temple of Amun before marriage and banged anyone they pleased consequence-free. A raging party would follow with no hard feelings.

Recently discovered hieroglyphs show the most famous and least significant pharaoh King Tutankhamen Tut to Bang. King Tut was only nine when he came to power and ruled until his death at nineteen from too much eating and fornicating. Classic example of nepotism gone awry, like electing a sex-crazed teenager with the munchies to the White House. Wars were lost, commodities dwindled, and the economy went flaccid while Tut banged every Egyptian hottie he could wrap his papyrus around. Egypt started wars they couldn't win so Tut could pillage enough ethnic food and sex slaves. Hey, the dude liked variety. Tut met his maker Ra as a result of breaking his leg showing off racing chariots. Don't worry too much about the ancient spoiled douche-nozzle: his dying wish to become immortal came true. King Tut's far more capable predecessors' and successors' names are forgotten by history, but we will always recognize that he was buried with his jewels and his bitches.

BIBLICAL TIMES 2200 BC–1 AD

The Book of Genesis in the Old Testament makes the world seem like a filthy, vile place full of plague, pestilence, and worst of all, buggery. But the food doesn't sound that bad. Genesis 1-12:

> The earth brought forth vegetation, plants yielding seed after their kind, and trees bearing fruit with seed in them, after their kind; and God saw that it was good.

Every food described in the Bible is nutritious and awesome. Grapes, pomegranates, and honey are marketed today as cure-alls for cancer, dementia, and being fat. The apple Eve ate in the Garden of Eden cleaned her teeth, gave her much needed fiber, and taught us all the pleasures of original sin. Wine always pairs well with religious fervor. Granted the forty years Moses spent in the desert eating stale, sand-filled, unleavened bread waiting for a text message from God was a raw deal.

Hanky-panky runs throughout the Old and New Testaments. Israelites like King Solomon were all about polygamy and concubines. The barren Sarah cheered her husband Abraham on as he banged her handmaid. Innkeepers were more than happy to offer their daughters and gay sons to distinguished guests. The Canaanites had holy consecrated hookers who dressed up in jewelry, makeup, and perfume. Don't get me started on the hail and brimstone of Sodom and Gomorrah. Worry not, for immortal sin will never go out of style.

We have Jesus to thank for that. Previous civilizations celebrated their gods' sexual ways, but Jesus was one chaste motherfucker. It must have been easy to abstain when you roll with a sausage party of twelve. Jesus used his gift of the gab and ability to cure syphilitic blindness to seduce his crew of apostles, who later died spreading his word. JC technically never banged anyone. But if speculation about his affair and subsequent child with Mary Magdalene are true, you know a sensitive guy like Jesus Cooked to Bang. Imagine Jesus combining his star power with the ability to whip up a Mediterranean aphrodisiac platter of figs, honey, and seafood served with water turned into wine. Slam-dunk conversion.

CHINA 1600 BC–PRESENT

Ancient Chinese did not eat to live; they lived to eat (always hungry an hour later). Long before Jesus converted water into wine, Chinese ancestors converted simple foods into feasts. The Chinese perfected pan-frying, flash-frying, deep-frying, stir-frying, steaming, stewing, and hot-boxing opium. They experimented with flavors, using mushrooms, sesame oil, cinnamon, star anise, chili peppers, garlic, ginger, and tiger cock. They rocked noodles thousands of years before the Italians "discovered" pasta. Shantung, Tientsin, and Peking cooks in the north made oily food like dumplings and steamed buns; Hunan, Szechwan, and Canton cooks in the south used spices, rice, and fresh vegetables. Much like today, Chinese ancestors strived for perfection in food presentation. We could all learn a thing or two from the Chinese.

We recognize ancient China's influence on civilization, science, and food. But they rarely get props for their innovations of the sexual variety. The early Taoists believed banging was the duty of man and woman. Women have bottomless yin essence; Men have finite yang essence. It was the man's duty to take some of the woman's yin by getting her off repeatedly before blowing his load. Failure to pleasure your lady resulted in health problems and death. Heed this ancient warning about the danger of blue balls. But then conservative Confucianism led to confusion: two hundred years of banging for procreation not recreation. Thank Buddha, though. The fabled Yellow Emperor inspired the nation to revert back to Taoism—and bang multiple women.

The Yellow Emperor's player days allowed him to achieve his goal of immortality. In life, the Yellow Emperor was a proponent of healthy living through good diet, martial arts, and banging. The dude lived to be one hundred years old and sired twenty-five children with the hottest women in China. Nobody in ancient China Cooked to Bang like him. When he wasn't fighting battles against four-armed monsters, he was mainlining yin. He served the foxiest Chinese ancestors homemade dim sum loaded with aphrodisiacs like ginger and seafood. In death, the Yellow Emperor became half dragon and ascended to heaven to become a god. He inspired billions of future Chinese people to Cook to Bang. Much respect.

PRE-COLUMBIAN AMERICA 1200 BC–1521 AD

The Spanish conquistadores and trailblazing Franciscan priests discovered the complex civilizations of the Aztecs, Mayans,

Incans, and Moche who governed themselves millennia before anyone ever heard of Jesus. Maize was the main crop that fueled these vastly different empires. The Aztecs chowed on tomatoes, avocados, tortillas, chiles, roast dog, and most of all chocolatl. This hot cacao drink flavored with vanilla beans turbocharged the rulers' libidos. Long before Taco Bell, the Mayans wrapped their beans, squash, turkey, and chiles up in tortillas, forming the original burrito. The Incans kicked ass at storing, preserving, and distributing their foods. They drank more alcoholic chicha than water and chewed coca leaves making them a drunk, coked-up force of nature. These ancient cultures laid down the foundation for modern Latin American cuisine.

The pre-Columbian cultures enjoyed a kinky existence before Cortez's cock-blocking conquistadores wiped them out with smallpox and the Bible. The Spaniards destroyed the culture, using fear of eternal damnation to get the 20 percent not exterminated to renounce their sinful ways. The Mayans worshipped masturbation and anal and oral sex. Young men were apprenticed in the art of banging by older women, the Mayan Mrs. Robinsons. Incan soldiers were sex-crazed maniacs high on maca, making them fierce in battle and explosive in the sack. The paintings and sculptures found on the pots of the Moche of Peru depict shit kinkier than most fetish porn sites. Women are jerking off or blowing skeletons with massive boners. Swallowing semen was essential to the birthing process and oh so nutritious (for the record, it still is). And who could forget the violent Aztec culture with polygamy, a goddess for prostitutes, and homosexuality as the mainstream?

Wild man Montezuma was the last Aztec emperor and had himself a genuine god complex. The guy was the pimp of his era, with a massive harem of wives, mistresses, and sex slaves. Satisfying that many ladies required fifty-two cups of chile-spiced hot chocolate a day to keep him humping and pumping. It's easy to see why Cortez was able to conquer the Aztecs. Montezuma was too slaphappy from all the cooking and banging. But ask yourself who had the better life. Cortez had an army of burly soldiers and prissy priests. Montezuma was covered in gold, drunk on chocolate, and knee-deep in Mesoamerican muff.

ANCIENT GREECE 1100 BC–50 BC

Ancient Greece boasted an impressive food culture that is recognizable today as the Mediterranean diet. Poseidon served up plenty of fish from the sea; Demeter provided aphrodisiacal crops like olives, grapes, figs, artichokes, and asparagus; Dionysus was kind enough to give the Greeks wine to philosophize and party with; Zeus was too busy creating things he could bang. The Greek legacy for great thinking was fueled by bread, olive oil, and wine. Part of that legacy involves the development of flavors using herbs and spices. The Greeks boast the original celebrity chefs, who regarded food as an art to honor the gods.

Ancient Greece was an advanced culture that was totally G-A-Y. Men worshipped the penis and assumed women were just jealous of their johnsons. Early Greek art depicts men with massive hard-ons and women fully dressed, if depicted at all. Zeus created the other gods using his schlong as a womb. Straight sex was engaged in for the sake of creating more males for the homo-machismo machine. Men owned everything and the very presence of women was a hindrance to the ultimate form of love: man-boy (aged twelve to fourteen). Doggy-style was the favored sexual position in Athens . . . some things never change. The straight men in ancient Greece sure loved their hookers. Prostitution was a mainstream profession, ranging from streetwalkers to the most expensive holy whores found in temples. Aphrodite was the goddess of banging while her uglier sister Athena, her tits covered by poisonous snakes, was the goddess of wisdom, aka cock-blocking.

Hercules became an immortal player that made the ladies go Greek. He was one of Zeus's countless illegitimate kids from hot mortal women, so his daddy's wife Hera hated him. The bee-yotch made many fruitless assassination attempts and tricked him into killing his own kids. Hercules did his penance, knocking down twelve ridiculous tasks, including slaying a lion, capturing monsters, shoveling an exponential pile of horseshit, and jumping on the homely grenade for his buddies, sport-fucking Medussa. This muscle-bound demigod had all manner of unattainable women. A little known fact is that Hercules was as great a chef as he was a warrior. Ever hear of the sheep with the Golden Fleece? Hercules sported it as a coat and made mint-flavored lamb chops for Aphrodite and her sexy entourage on Mount Olympus. Hera was out of town at a crabby bitch goddess convention. Mount Olympus was a rocking with the screams of pleasure that became thunder and lightning in the Grecian sky.

INDIA 1000 BC–PRESENT

Every moment of religious significance for Buddhists, Hindus, and Muslims on the subcontinent of India was fueled by rice and wheat. Chapatis (unleavened wheat bread cooked on skillet) fed the ancestors of the array of cultures that went on to create karma, dharma, vishnas, dogmas, and doggy-style. Dairy products like ghee and cheese curds were so essential to the early Hindu diet they stopped slaughtering and started worshipping cows. No more sexy time with Bessie either. The Koran forbade

Muslims to eat pork so pigs were off the table, too. The Jains won't eat food that casts a shadow. Vegetarians ruled the day. That doesn't mean Indian ancestors ate boring foods; Indians are resourceful. Long dead and reincarnated chefs made simple ingredients like rice and veggies into flavorful feasts using cinnamon, cardamom, and mace. These Grand Poobah spices became India's principal exports. Indian food remains to this day bold in spice and rich with history.

India's sex history isn't too shabby. Kama Sutra anyone? This Sanskrit text with graphic illustrations of fisting, double-teaming, and other family-friendly activities remains history's finest sex ed book. Ancient Indians studied sex like a science. (I like to think I'm carrying on that tradition.) Getting your partner off was a sacred duty. Orgiastic fertility rituals were common, while polygamy and hedonism were lifestyles expected of people in power. It's good to be the king . . . or maharaja! Tantric sex was developed for people eager to gain enlightenment through banging. But those dipshit British imperialists turned the cold shower on kinky Kama Sutra culture. Repressive morals are the norm for the modern, conservative Indian populace. Ironically, the Kama Sutra and the ancient Indian sex culture are now embraced by the modern Western world.

Centuries later, Mahatma Gandhi united his countrymen to kick the British's uptight bums out of India. History remembers him as a man of peace and diplomacy. Rarely do we give him props for being a player. Ghandi's political career almost capsized over photos of him in bed with five hot naked girls. But the smooth operator played it off like it was an experiment to test his celibacy. Try that excuse next time you get caught in bed with someone else. India's loinclothed lothario used his power and charisma to rack up and shack up with the sexiest ladies in his nonviolence movement. Gandhi's ashram was no doubt a revolving door of satisfied Cook to Bang customers. He may have been a vegetarian, but you know there was one meat Gandhi went to town on.

ROMAN EMPIRE 509 BC–312 AD

Roman civilization ripped off the Greek culture and religion and slapped their own fancy names on them. They raped and marauded the world so its people could stuff their fat faces with spoils from conquered lands. That meant culinary innovation. Elite Romans enjoyed extravagant vittles like peacock brains and lark tongue; common Romans still enjoyed three-course meals with veggies, meat, and desserts. Ancient Rome was a wine-soaked orgy of excess. They drank morning, day, and night, yet still managed to modernize the ancient world. Romans were organized, but they partied down. Feasts would last for hours, sometimes days with twelve-course meals complemented by dancing, theater, comedy, and bloody gladiator battles. These hard-partying Romans would go to the vomitorium, chow down, and then yak up their food to make room for more. When it was all over, they sat around drinking, gambling, and screwing.

The Romans couldn't help their whorish nature. They inherited their Cook to Bang culture from the Etruscans whose land they had conquered. Etruscan women were famed for giving it up to men besides their husbands, often in public ceremonies that were nothing short of orgy feasts. Voyeurism, partner-swapping, and gymnastic sexual positions were par for the course. Etruscans were never sure of the paternity of their kids so the village raised them together. Methinks our culture could learn a few things from the Etruscans. The Romans certainly did. Orgy culture as seen in the film *Caligula* was prevalent behind palace walls. Wealthy Roman men had slave girls to feed them grapes among other nibbles. Emperor Claudius XXXIX's wife loved to gangbang. The tramp snuck out of the palace into commoners' brothels to be ridden hard and put away wet. Nero was the original furry, dressing up in animal pelts and ravishing sex slaves tied to stakes. The freaky frescoes found in the ruins of Pompeii are a window into Rome's sexual soul.

No Roman embodied the decadence of ancient Rome like famed general and consummate player Mark Antony. In his youth, Antony fled gambling debts in Rome to Greece where he emulated local god Dionysus by drinking and screwing everything. He knocked up and abandoned his first of five wives to become his cousin Emperor Julius Caesar's BFF. Antony was up shit's creek when his cuz was assassinated so he seduced his way into Cleopatra's Nile. Under the guise of discussing trade, Cleopatra was plied with the finest Roman wines and cheese. Mark Antony Cooked to Bang his way into getting Egypt to back his campaign to retake Rome. Too bad Octavian (later renamed Augustus) wanted Mark's head on a platter for marrying, knocking up, and then abandoning his sister for sluttier pastures in Egypt. Mark Antony and Cleopatra killed themselves to avoid admitting failure. Antony's legacy is destroying the Roman Empire and siring seven legitimate kids, plus countless bastards from whom descended famed perverts like Caligula and Nero.

NATIVE AMERICANS 500 BC–PRESENT

The Pilgrims of Plymouth Rock would have been FUBAR without the help of the Wampanoag tribe. Native Americans had North America well sorted from coast to coast before the white man handed them blankets laced with smallpox and herpes. Each tribe had unique customs and diet. The New England tribes fished; the Midwest tribes hunted; the Southeast tribes farmed. Corn or maize (meaning "life") was the centerpiece of all tribes' diets. Native Americans thanked their respective gods for the handout and honored the animals they killed, using every part of the carcasses. The cuisine wasn't fancy by European standards. They ate one-course meals without pomp or circumstance. But hospitality was at their culture's core. There was always food for even the poorest member of a tribe.

The Pilgrims were grateful for their benefactors-in-loincloths' hospitality. But the Native American raw sexuality offended conservative palefaces. It seems these hospitable heathens never heard of Jesus Christ or original sin. Native Americans viewed sex as a part of nature. The balance of male and female energy was necessary for cosmic harmony. They engaged in erotic ritual dances, masturbation, polygamy, and casual sex. Virginity was neither celebrated nor encouraged. The Native American women loved to bang and enjoyed many partners, white men included.

Pocahontas was one such minx who preferred men of the vanilla variety. We're talking about a liberated woman way ahead of her time. When Pocahontas saw a man she wanted to bang she went for it. John Smith didn't have a chance when Pocahontas invited him into her wigwam to discuss diplomacy. Smith expected her tribal chief father and his advisers to be at the table. Instead he found a clambake for two and a horny heathen hottie. Pocahontas Cooked to Bang John Smith and they fell in love. Too bad Smith's fellow countrymen were raging dickheads who stole Pocahontas's land and clambake recipe.

JAPAN 300 BC–PRESENT

The Japanese have always savored the abundant seafood in the surrounding sea, the mysterious and delicious vegetables and roots from the mountain, and rice rice rice! Ancient feudal lords' power was not based on the number of heads they lopped off with a samurai sword, but on the amount of rice they controlled. You weren't nobody if you couldn't feed your people. The Japanese diet has been producing hot women for over two thousand hard-bodied years. They shun fats and oils, eat little meat, and chow down on vegetables. Rice-based sake was the drink of choice. Noodles and other Chinese imports became integral in the later era, but in distinct Japanese fashion. The Japanese foods we know and love, like sushi, tempura, and yakitori are modern interpretations on ancient Japanese meals.

Props to the Japanese ancestors for influencing their modern descendants' wacky perversions. Sumo-on-midget porn, bukkake, and used teenage girls' panties sold in subway vending machines wouldn't be possible without the island nation's rich history of freaky freaking. The Japanese are hip to the fact that sex does not equate sin. Sex is a sacred part of Japan's native religion, Shintoism. Feminists bristle because Japanese culture is all about satisfying the urges of men. Ancient samurai wives were trained to sexually satiate their husbands so they could fight better. Good oral was the secret to keeping their men out of the bedchambers of courtesans, geisha, and prostitutes. That is why all men want to date Japanese girls.

Being a samurai in ancient Japan was a pretty kick-ass way to live. Just ask sixteenth-century swordsman and lady-killer Miyamoto Musashi. He was an upstart samurai who dropped bombs on Hiroshima many centuries before World War II. He was such a bonafide badass that he stopped dueling with a real sword because of his massive body count. Miyamoto always made time for the ladies between kicking samurai ass. It was on whenever he served females of nobility cherry blossom tea and sashimi. He never spent a night alone with his harem attending to all his wounds. Miyamoto Musashi Cooked to Bang like a true warrior.

COLONIAL AMERICA 1607–1776

The original Americans were the best fed people on the planet thanks to the Native Americans they later dicked over. The colonists enjoyed a bounty of beef, mutton, turkey, duck, salmon, eels, oysters, and fish. Too bad they squandered these culinary gems by creating tavern culture, the original sports bars. These establishments served crappy food like stews and stale bread at a flat rate. But they lured in the underrepresented colonialists with beer and rum to enjoy while conspiring against the crown. Boozing has always been as American as apple pie eaten off Betsy Ross's tits. The Declaration of Independence was signed in Philadelphia's famed City Tavern over oodles of brew be-tween games of quarters. It makes you wonder if Thomas Jefferson's eloquent words were written under the influence of outrage or booze.

The New England Puritans sucked the fun right out of this new, exciting land like my born-again uncle does at Thanksgiving. Theo-fascism ruled the day. Laws were written against sodomy, adultery, and good old-fashioned fornication. Premarital sex was punished with beatings, imprisonment, and worse, forced marriage. Virginity was a premium, yet engaged couples fornicated long before their weddings. Extramarital affairs were the greatest abomination. Just ask poor Hester Prynne and her bastard wild child Pearl from Nathanial Hawthorne's *The*

Scarlet Letter. Lucky for liberated modern Americans, the Puritans lightened up when they united with the more lax colonies to become Yankees against the British. After achieving independence, the right to birth control and consequence-free sexy time was granted by the Supreme Court.

Benjamin Franklin was the colonies' master statesman and cunning linguist who charmed the pantaloons off the court of Versailles. Louis XVI agreed to support the colonial bitch-slapping of the English back across the Atlantic. This tactical alliance allowed the colonies to become the United States of America. Prudish historians forget that Franklin was a first-class player who banged his way through Versailles' vixens. The low-key lady-slayer returned home with an encyclopedic knowledge of wining, dining, and sixty-nining. He also brought the art of Cooking to Bang to his people and weaned his fellow Americans off imported British wines with a homegrown variety. Ben hosted his share of ladies for aphrodisiac feasts of New England lobster and Chesapeake Bay oysters and crab. And you wonder why Ben Franklin is on the hundred dollar bill.

FRENCH REVOLUTION 1638–1799

Benjamin Franklin enjoyed himself gallivanting with the Versailles Court. Can you blame the guy who went from crappy tavern food to elegant multicourse feasts with lascivious ladies powdered up and ready to party? The peasants starved, paying unreasonable royal taxes, but inside the walls of Versailles it was party time. This grand evolution of food began with the Sun King Louis XIV. He was a royal fatso with an army of chefs that piled food high in multiple courses. New World foods like chocolate were en vogue as were oysters, the Viagra of the day. His great-grandson Louis XV took over the throne and followed up his culinary legacy with more opulence, focus on service and presentation. Eight-course meals, each containing eight dishes, equaling sixty-four dishes, were the norm. Louis XV starved his own people and enriched himself by exporting French grains and then importing them at ten times the price. Can you blame the starving peasants for revolting?

Louis XVI continued the fuck-the-poor tradition he inherited from his grandfather. He was a glutton like Louis XIV, but a total pussy with debilitating sexual dysfunction. His wife, Marie Antoinette, was the hottest piece of ass in Europe, yet he couldn't get it up and consummate the marriage. Louis's flaccid libido was the subject of court gossip. Louis XV demanded updates on his sex life until his dying breath and Marie Antoinette's brother even coached the milquetoast king on how to bang his sister like a man. Imagine your grandpa and brother-in-law armchair quarterbacking your screwing technique. So what's a foxy and fashionable girl like Marie Antoinette to do? Gangbang men and women alike of course. One of Marie Antoinette's crimes warranting her execution was being a total cum Dumpster. Apparently Madame Deficit's food orgies were distasteful to the starving peasants who never had a chance to eat her cake.

Too bad Louis XVI never had this book. *Cook to Bang* would have thawed the iceberg between his wife's legs. Their marriage was political; sexual attraction was its casualty. It was like a terminal blind date. The check never comes and you are stuck listening to boring stories about your date's cats. But imagine if Louis had the good sense to seduce her. He could have invited Marie into his chambers with a nice cheese plate and wine. Louis XVI never demonstrated to Marie that he was not a boy, but a virile man with a musket in his pocket. Perhaps France would still have a royal family if Louis had grown a pair. Instead, his wife banged his friends and mocked his tiny package behind his back.

HISTORICAL COOK-TO-BANG OFF

Which super-pimp would win out in a Cook to Bang *Iron Chef*–style throw-down, with history's finest pieces of ass on the line?

Marilyn Monroe: Marco Polo *vs.* Jesus

Diamonds (and downers) were this girl's best friend. Marco Polo was a wealthy merchant trading spices from around the globe; Jesus was a holy carpenter. You do the math.

Joan of Arc: King Tut *vs.* Pocahontas

Joan of Arc didn't dig dudes, especially royal douches like King Tut. Sexually liberated Pocahontas would poke-a-hottie and serve up some post- scissoring cornmeal fritters.

Helen of Troy: Gilgamesh *vs.* Musashi

These bloodthirsty maniacs would hack each other to pieces with paring knives long before either could chop up a Greek salad for the woman thousands of Trojans (not condoms, fool) died for.

Cleopatra: Ben Franklin *vs.* Hercules

Hercules was hung like a demigod. But Cleopatra would never have lost her kingdom with our man Ben's diplomacy and mastery of French cooking. Plus, he'd probably invent a vibrator for her. Mark Antony could only watch.

Marie Antoinette: Yellow Emperor *vs.* Montezuma

These legendary cocksmen would both win. Marie was always down for a Gaul gangbang so long as it was catered.

> **The Vestal Virgins: Ghandi *vs*. Louis XVI**
> Ghandi would bang every last one, claiming it was a test of faith; impotent Louis would piss his pantaloons in shame while the ladies would trade their V cards for vegetarian delights.

These historical figures were each able to pull off the implausible, improbable, and downright impossible. But don't let cock-blocking historians say you can't be Herculean in the sack. There is greatness in all of us. Chances are you lack immortality, an army that can be mobilized at your whim, and jewels to throw at any hot piece of ass. But you have this book: you must utilize tools like *Cook to Bang* to achieve your baser goals, in spite of your historical insignificance. Who's to say that some blind bard with a lute at Ye Olde Renaissance Faire won't sing of your bawdy antics centuries from now? Read on to find out how to induct yourself into the *Cook to Bang* hall of fame.

3

Cook to Bang War Room

You must strategize your Cook to Bang endgame and know how to get there. It is like a road map or navigation system that guides you to your destination. Without a clear set of directions, you could end up lost, confused and crying in the dark. Don't be that guy washing dishes in your kitchen at 11 P.M. wondering, "What the fuck just happened?" Anything worth accomplishing takes patience and planning. To truly conquer you must know your conquest. That requires legwork. But don't worry, you lazy fucker. The extra effort is minimal. Those who have spent an entire weekend in bed can assure you the payoff is worth the price of admission.

TAP THAT GOAL'S ASS

You need to know what you want and then figure out how to get it. Successful people like Bill Gates, Hugh Hefner, and even *Girls Gone Wild* uber-douche Joe Francis set their sights high and went for it. Haters told them it was impossible: "No way in hell can you corner the computer market!" "You're crazy if you think you can make a fortune off getting hot women to pose naked." "You're a tool and a fool to think you can get rich exploiting college girls' low self-esteems with chintzy Mardi Gras beads so they'll show you their tits." Here's a little insider knowledge for you: I worked at a talent agency that turned down the opportunity to sign Joe Francis and represent *Girls Gone Wild*. They said his project wasn't commercial enough. Fast-forward to today: the agency is out of business; Joe Francis owns his own island.

This principle remains true in dating. You can get someone deemed "unattainable" using the right approach and execution. Bear in mind that there are some who are too famous, too rich, or too married. But the determined and clever can get past even those roadblocks. The important thing is to never sell yourself short. Don't settle for that bloated bar tramp offering blowjobs in the toilet stall for shots of Jägermeister. We've all compromised our standards in a drunken, desperate state. Like a scooter, skanks are fun to ride until your friends see you on one. You deserve better! Focus and be realistic.

Being realistic doesn't mean settling. Never, ever settle. You won't have to with your charm, talents, and cooking skills. Settling is for the chump who ten years from now has a beached manatee they call a spouse on their couch watching daytime TV. Being realistic means managing your expectations. A *Maxim* model won't bang the kid with acne who lives in his mom's basement and works at Subway for eight dollars an hour. The poor kid can whack it to his heart's content, but she will not jump off the page to give him a happy ending. But she might finish *you* off, dear reader.

Much of what can be achieved carnally during a date is tele-graphed during courtship. You can shape your goals by under-standing what's been communicated when you first meet them, and later when you set the date up. More on that in chapter 8,

Setting the Bait. For now, just know that you should hoover up details to exploit later. Read the signs like a South American shaman and be the triumphant leader of the village. Just don't compromise your status or comfort.

We all have limits. What will you put up with to get what you want? Have you ever found yourself giving your intended conquest's fat drunk friend a ride home? Did this fat drunk friend puke in your car then try to kiss you with blown chunks on her breath? When you rejected her, did she then try to jump out of your car while it was moving? Did this same vile girl refuse to tell you where she lived for another thirty minutes? And after all that, when you got back to your intended conquest's home, was she asleep and no longer up for it? True story. My limits were defied, my car reeked of vomited-caked regret, and I had to soak my blue balls in ice. My advice is to know your limits when it comes to financial, physical, and time-related matters. This tragedy cost me a pricey trip to the car wash, utter disgust, and left me dead tired for work the next day. Was this girl amazing enough to be worth the trouble? Is crack non-addictive?

So ask yourself, "Are they worth it?" Bringing someone into your home to cook for them is a big deal. Quality control is essential. Yes, Cooking to Bang does save you money, time, and frustration. But it will be considerably more expensive than a restaurant should your date go *Fatal Attraction* on your ass. Just because he or she was rendered temporarily insane by the devil or Jesus is no excuse . . . unless they are an incredible piece of ass. Then I'd almost tolerate bunnies boiled in my favorite stockpot. Psychopaths are the best lovers. That is a moral quandary I leave to you to make sense of. You may have satisfied your short-term goal of getting some tail, but your long-term goal of not dying at the hands of a homicidal nymphomaniac could be shit-canned.

SHORT-TERM OBJECTIVE

Know up front what you want out of your night. What can be achieved physically and/or emotionally by the end of the evening? Have a clear and tangible benchmark to shoot for, but also know what you will settle for. It is like those "vision boards" used in *The Secret*. But instead of the dream of white picket fences, a Mercedes, or smiling children, you should have snapshots from your favorite pornos. Visualize yourself rocking doggy-style, exchanging oral affection, and making the Religious Right gasp.

Remember there is always next time when pursuing your short-term goals. Yes, you should try to get as much play as you can. But never push too hard. This can cut short a perfect evening, or worse, get your ass kicked or thrown in jail. *Cook to Bang* advocates allowing things to unfold naturally. If they don't, that girl or guy isn't worth your time anyhow. Being aggressive like a rabbit on PCP will leave a sour taste in your date's mouth. Your reputation among future conquests could devolve from Kitchen Casanova to Chester the Molester.

Obviously being considered a borderline rapist is a no-no. But don't be a pussy about satisfying your short-term goals, either. Your campaign is screwed if you don't land a kiss at the very least. Hesitate to make a move and you'll never escape the "friend" penalty box. If you like listening to your "friend" bitch about the assholes that bang them and never call again, you're in luck! But that asshole was supposed to be you. You have plenty of friends already. You don't need some hot number reminding you that you can't close the deal. There is no cure for making the wrong impression. Move on.

Knowing what kind of impression you want to make is crucial. What goes on in their head as they leave that night, or if you're lucky, in the morning, will determine where things transpire. Leave them marveling about your skills in cooking, conversation, and kissing. Leave them wanting more. Become their heroin, their sexual fix. They should be desperate for round two, three, and fourteen hundred. Plant a seed in their head that will sprout down into their crotch.

Not every seed blossoms into the kind of fruit you want to eat. Sometimes it rots like a moldy orange. *Cook to Bang* encourages you to visualize and achieve your short-term goals, but accept it when shit goes sour and move on. Don't stress it too much. You might discover that your date is a prude who doesn't kiss on the first date. Cut your losses and erase their phone number. Anybody who isn't going to play tonsil hockey on the first date is not banging you on the second. I wouldn't even get your hopes up for your church-sanctioned honeymoon. Next!

LONG-TERM OBJECTIVE

Ignore this section if you plan on never seeing your date again; one-night stands can be a beautiful thing. Or the sex just sucked. It could have been eternity from the time when you come and they go. Or it could have been such a toxic or shameful experience that you roofied yourself so you'd forget the night ever happened.

But what if your short-term objective panned out exactly as you planned? Now what? Where do you see the two of you the day after? What about next week? Next month? Next year? I'm all for spontaneity, but you should project long term. You don't want to get caught with your pants down somewhere down the line. Only a sucker will let the world sodomize them while they're distracted by all the pretty colors. This assessment is for your own benefit.

First determine an appropriate follow-up course of action. So you cooked a mind-blowing meal that evolved into a night of unspeakable acts of lust. You are keen for the unrated sequel. Play it cool. Don't let temptation override logic. Never kiss and tell, even if you think it won't get back to them. It will. Don't shoot yourself in the nuts by calling them the next day. Leave room for mystery and suspense. Let the tension build over a couple days so they wonder if you are going to call. When you finally do reach out, be subtle and noncommittal. A simple e-mail, text message, or Facebook message works best. Don't mention the banging and do not under any circumstances contact them again until they reciprocate. Shoot the shit when you connect before you set up another date. If you couldn't convince them to come to your pad before, now is your chance!

Now get out your kinky vision board again. By all means, keep your porno images up, but revise the board with new knowledge and insights. You have a better idea of what this date will or won't do. Perhaps they revealed a bisexual streak that could lead to some enticing mathematical possibilities. Develop your long-term objective for this relationship. Be honest and realistic. Delusions of grandeur will only set you up for crushing defeat and creating stalkerish collages wearing a filthy bathrobe. NEVER discuss any of this with the person in question. Discussing the relationship, or DTR, is the kiss of death. DTR=RIP. But it is important to have a clear vision in your own mind. Then navigate the relationship into what you deem he or she is qualified for.

One-Night Stand

As mentioned above, this is a one-time deal. Chances are regret and self-loathing will soon follow. Enjoy it for whatever it was worth. You may learn something. At the very least you should raise your standards for future sexcapades. But perhaps you're a straight-up player. You have no interest in seeing this midnight marauder again on principle. There ain't enough time to bang someone more than once with your roster. Add another notch to your bedpost. Chances are cooking won't even factor into this one. That means no dishes to wash!

Booty Call

You both are clear that this relationship is based on banging. You probably don't even like each other. The only thing either of you are interested in is the next time you see each other naked. You rarely speak before 11 P.M., and never sober. There are a few unfortunate souls who think that a booty call is something more than emotionless sex. A word to the wise: if someone only calls you after midnight drunk, looking to bang then you are a booty call, probably one of many. Accept it. You will never have to cook them dinner, let alone buy them food. Arrange things right and they will leave immediately after so you can get your beauty rest.

Friends with Benefits

A friend with benefits, aka fuck buddy, is like a booty call except you actually like this person . . . as a friend. You don't mind being seen in public together, but you don't want people to know you're dancing the horizontal mambo. These relationships evolve from a friendship that became more after one too many cocktails. You both laugh it off as a mistake, but the seal has been broken so dipping into each other's salsa again is fair game. The problem is someone usually develops feelings beyond lust. Humans are possessive. Don't be surprised if your fuck buddy gets pissy when you date someone new. The friendship based on years of mutual interest and respect could disintegrate. I've had some incredible romps with women I remain close to. But others now regard me as protoplasm lower on the evolutionary scale than scabies.

Dating

Hanging out and banging someone does not mean you are in a committed relationship. Cook to Bang freely. You are nonexclusive, like a free-agent athlete, able to date a whole stable of hotties without owing any of them an explanation. The fact you were out until 4 A.M. and reek of perfume is none of their business. This relationship is like a thirty-day money-back guarantee at RadioShack. You can sample the merchandise, but you will need to return them or accept them as a permanent fixture in your life. Bang each other's brains out in the meantime. You can observe their good and bad traits in their natural habitat. They might reveal they are in a cult or, worse, fart in front of you. You can gauge if they are a picky eater (high maintenance), willing to try new things (up for a threesome), and if they are good company (not a bitch or wanker) with little damage to your wallet. A date that expects you to take out a second mortgage to pay for dinner is not relationship material anyway.

Relationship

Congratulations! You found someone who rocks your world. You're off the market and you sent the other skanks packing.

This special someone loves your company, passions, and the food you cook. You introduce them as your girlfriend or boyfriend without hesitation. You would rather spend time with them than your best friend, favorite sibling, and even your dog. You rarely go out now since the objective of finding someone to bang is complete. Cuddling is no longer some obligatory motion you perform to score round two of banging. Choose this person carefully. Never settle. Be sure to get your inner slut out of your system. A wandering eye can be like a syphilitic monkey that won't stop pulling out your pubic hair until you scratch that itch. We've all ended up in some relationship we view as a slightly better alternative to cancer. Commit wisely. Remember what Johnnie Cochran says, "If the glove don't fit, you must acquit that bitch and find one who gives better head."

MANIPULATION = PERSUASION

Cooking to Bang is an art. Critics call it a manipulative art. And you know what? They're right. You must become a manipulative bastard to get what you want. You may feel that this is not your true self. But Darwin taught us that one must adapt or go extinct. Survival of the sexually fittest. There is no fruit basket for second place (perhaps a bottle of lotion). But why settle? That's for the "nice guys" who play by the rules. The opposite sex always games you; game back. That is sexual power. You are leveling the playing field. Like the ancient philosopher Fleetwood Mac sang, "Players only love you when they're playing."

Never be up front about your ultimate goal . . . merely to bang. That would leave you without so much as a pair of panties to sniff. Completing your objectives means subtle manipulation. People who tell you they enjoy delaying pleasure are liars.

They just can't close the deal and are justifying themselves. But that's not your problem, is it? You're a closer.

Wearing the right mask is an important step in manipulation. I have pretended to be many things in the name of banging: massage therapist, rock star, gynecologist. I sport-fucked a pro-life right-wing Christian activist in college to see if I could. This girl publicly condemned people like me to hell so I ingratiated myself with her clan. I baked cookies, came up with catchy slogans like "What Would Jesus Abort?", and pretended to pray with them. She came over to my house to discuss an upcoming protest at a Planned Parenthood clinic. I made her pasta and then made my move. You might assume she was saving herself for Jesus. But no, she had her own set of anal beads. I banged the bejesus out of her, but declined her offer to "pulverize my sphincter." Later she wanted to discuss our relationship to which I replied, "What relationship?" She stormed out, cursed me to hell, and said she never wanted to see me again.

Game, set, and match.

For those of you concerned, I insisted on using a condom considering her stance on abortion. You have to wonder if this holy roller would have carried my demon seed.

While I don't recommend going to that extreme, you can be subtle and still move mountains. That is what Cook to Bang is all about. In a way, cooking is a false front. You could almost leave your German scheisse porn on the coffee table (don't do that, more on this later in chapter 9, Pregame to Bang), but once they taste your strudel, they'll be telling all their friends how sensitive you are. Let them believe you are the type of person they want their parents to meet. (For my part, I hope to never meet the parents of some girl I'm just banging. Visions of a girl's father chasing me down the street with his nine iron still haunt my dreams.)

You must love to bang a lot, too, if you bought this book. Remember that without the banging, Cook to Bang is an exercise in futility. Just don't seem like you're wooing. Play it cool. Never be too nice or too evil. Manipulate the situation like Machiavelli. Banging should seem like a spontaneous accident. You both can laugh it off while you are panting and drenched in sweat. "One thing led to another and suddenly we were sixty-nining on the dining room table. We're so silly!"

THE ART OF WAR

A Cook to Bang chef is a wartime general in the kitchen and bedroom. Never give up like Poland in World War II. Fight until your last dying breath. Get what you want by any means necessary. Nothing can stop you if you play it cool and smart. Use every weapon in your arsenal until the white flag of underwear is waved.

The battle begins long before your date shows up at your house for an innocent dinner. This is your final battle in a drawn-out war. Both sides are eager for a pleasant resolution. So please them. It's the least you can do as the victor. To the victor go the spoils. Spoil yourself. But be sure to spoil your captive, too.

It may seem ridiculous to consider your date an enemy. You may adore this person and perhaps see them as your future life partner. The art of war is about making your enemy your friend . . . or in this case your girlfriend or boyfriend. There will be a struggle for control, so take no prisoners. No apologies are necessary so long as you are a gracious and sensual ruler.

Know thy enemy before conquering their clothing. Be a

good listener. Exploit any tidbits they mention, like their neck being sensitive. Should they resist your advances, gently kiss the nape of said neck. If you are truly sinister, investigate online like a digital private eye.

> ### DIGITAL DICK
>
> Social networking sites like Facebook, Myspace, and Twitter are a treasure trove of insider trading info you can take advantage of. Get briefed on your date's passions, hatreds, and preferences like music, movies and food. To them, it will seem like serendipity that you, too, love steamed artichokes and are totally gay for saving the llamas of Peru.

Should you meet any resistance when conquering the territory in their pants, don't fight. If they pull away, push them out the door. If they get pushy or bitchy, pull away like you have better things to do than get teased. Watch them run back. They'll greet you as their sexual liberator. Your presence enriches their territory. Be ready for the standing O and undergarments being thrown at your feet.

SENDING THE RIGHT MESSAGE

You need to communicate effectively to get what you want out of life. Successful politicians connect with their constituency on a visceral level. Ronald Reagan is most remembered not for his policies, but for banging Gorbachev's wife in the Oval Office. But he was also a very good communicator! Success with your date comes down to communication. If you can't reach common ground, then you can't build a connection. Connect to bang.

Miscommunication is the cause of most wars. I'm not talking Cook to Bang art of war; I'm talking real wars. Wars where pain is inflicted worse than Heidi Montag releasing another album. I'm talking *Ill Communication*. You must avoid this if you are to pull off some sexual healing with a hot number considered out of your league.

Carry an air of nonchalance like it doesn't matter what happens during the date. It really doesn't. Some dates are prudes or have the personality of a goldfish. Don't beat yourself up should your goals flatline. Egos bruise like a banana in a Bangkok sex show, but you will experience more triumphs than you can count. And soon enough, that nonchalance won't be an act anymore. So make like you could take it or leave it. Not banging you is their loss. You have more pliable and sensual playmates.

The thing you should communicate with clarity and sincerity is that the date will be fun. You'll have fun regardless—the way you always do. Banging at the end of the date is even more fun, of course, and they will be more willing to head over to your sex lair when their guard is down.

NEVER, EVER OVERDO IT

Keep yourself in check when you Cook to Bang. The recipes in this book are engineered to be delicious and seductive, but also to look like you just threw them together. Overdo it and you will reek of desperation. And he who is too eager does not get laid. We've all had a date we waited for on the edge of our seat with delusions of grandeur (or handjobs) waltzing through our minds. You change your outfit ten times beforehand. There is a difference between scheming to bang and sweating irrelevant details like how your hair looks by candlelight. Your seduction should unfold like there was no other conclusion but you getting your freak on. Know that you deserve this and you will have it. And remember there's always a next time.

Don't set some impossible benchmark in the kitchen that you can't follow up. You might pull off a five-course dinner by candlelight, but now you've set an impossible standard for yourself. Chances are you will scare them off, and will be informed they are "joining a monastery first thing tomorrow." Save that clichéd romanticism for when you propose your undying love. Overdoing it will lead to waning interests. Keep it simple. Don't serve a hooker caviar.

4

Culinary Seduction Blueprints

Much of your Cook to Bang success comes down to planning the right menu. You should know what to cook for whom and why. Are you cooking a five-course meal or sticking to one course? How much time do you have to shop and prepare the meal? Prepare a meal based on your date's preferences to get the most bang for your buck.

A well-crafted culinary seduction is designed like an architectural gem. Your foundation is a killer entrée that holds your game all together. The walls are the appetizers to get them comfortable. Your game won't get rained out with your dessert roof. The charming accents, like curtains, are your culinary presentation, such as color and garnishes. Are you ready to build your dream house of ill repute?

PLANNING THE MEAL

Use your imagination in the kitchen. Humans are granted free will so that we can innovate, not imitate. Don't make something boring and predictable. You'd be better off microwaving a Hungry Man dinner or catching the five o'clock blue plate special with the geriatrics at Country Kitchen Buffet. Be bold with you palette! You will put your date to sleep serving spaghetti with sauce out of the jar. Those who cook without passion deserve to sleep alone. Be inspired and you will inspire your date—to get naked that is. Just don't cook weird food just to be weird. It's all about righteous food combinations.

Combining flavors and textures is an art. There's a reason why the great chefs of the world are regarded as celebrities. They are no different than the famed Renaissance artists. Culinary pioneers discover groundbreaking food combinations that become commonplace years, decades, centuries, and millennia later. The Earl of Sandwich blew his contemporaries' minds by asking for meat slapped between two slices of bread. His name is now synonymous with the most common lunch item on the planet. Discover your own groundbreaking food combos, but avoid the pitfalls.

Magical Food Combos

Figs and Brie	Seafood and mango
Chocolate and berries	Tuna and mayonnaise
Honey and lemon	Eggs and hot sauce
Beets and goat cheese	Chicken and rosemary
Chocolate and peanut butter	Balsamic vinegar and olive oil
Spinach and feta cheese	Cream cheese and honey
Dates and bacon	Asparagus and lemon
Turkey and cranberry	Ginger and any meat
Lime and cilantro	Garlic and butter
Basil and tomato	Avocado and anything

Unholy Couplings

Cheese and Asian foods	Milk and Dr Pepper
Cheese and ice cream	Marshmallows and vinegar
Ice cream and onions	Cookies and ketchup
Fruit and mayonnaise	Spam and anything
Peanut butter and mayonnaise	Pop Rocks and soda
Seafood and chocolate	

The number of courses you serve in a Cook to Bang meal will vary depending on numerous factors. It all comes down to how much time and money you are willing to put into shopping, prepping, cooking, and serving the food. Three courses is a good amount to impress: starter, entrée, and dessert. Four- or five-course meals reek of desperation. As discussed in the previous chapter, never overdo it. Sometimes an entrée is impressive on its own. You can class up a boring entrée with a killer starter that doesn't take long to create. One course could shine like a glorious sun orbited by complimentary side dishes.

Your meal should leave an impression. When I say meal, I mean the overall experience: food, conversation, and seduction. This date should be intrigued enough to bang you again and again. Make them feel lucky to be there. Impress the hell out of them so they tell their friends. Build a reputation for being an amazing cook and you can bang their friends in good time. A little known secret is that a crew of girls will bang the same dude out of innate competition. Don't question the logic, boys. Just go with it.

PRESENTATION

Expensive restaurants present their food like works of art. Presentation is as essential to culinary seduction as lube is for anal. You want the food to look as good as it tastes. This is a first impression. No mulligans. Guys: sweat the details because women take mental notes about the food just as they do about your pad. Your total tally will determine how the night ends up. A little extra effort pays off in moans and scratches on your back. Sweat the steamy details.

Food can taste amazing, but look like hot garbage. Your game will be screwed; you will not be. Picky eaters won't give you the benefit of the doubt and your handcrafted food will go colder than Glenn Beck at an orgy. Why go to the effort of cooking something practically fuckable if you are just going to toss it haphazardly on a plate? You could have been doing something more productive, like, say, getting neutered, since you ain't getting any no how.

By this rationale, you can get away with a disappointing meal by making it look pretty. Speaking from experience, chefs at fancy restaurants ruin the occasional meal. They don't always have time to remake the meal and risk alienating their demanding clientele. Instead they dress up the dish with distracting flare. Sure, it is style over content, but so is Western culture. Wow the shit out them and they might forget all about the dog kibble floating in their soup.

Food presentation comes down to layout. Any good dish will feature its main element, usually meat, with sides like starch or veggies. Use the items available to maximize presentation. Work with the colors you have to make it visually pleasing. If there a number of small items, arrange them in neat piles so they don't look jumbled. Lay a bed of rice, veggies, or noodles and place your main element, such as a chicken breast, on top. Place dipping sauces in their own containers in the middle of a plate surrounded by appetizers. Mix salads evenly so treats like cherry tomatoes, chunks of chicken, candied walnuts, and blue cheese crumbles are visible up top. Every dish should look like you thought it through even if it was just an afterthought. Keep it classy by default.

The easiest way to class up a meal is by garnishing the shit out of it. Garnishes are often irrelevant to the taste of the meal, but work wonders to leave an impression. This culinary bling brings color to a bland-looking dish and often provides a pleasant aroma. Anything organic can be a garnish so long as it compliments your meals. Many Asian cultures take garnishing to the extreme, creating paper lanterns out of radishes or an orchid out of a chili pepper. That is awesome, though overkill for a date.

Food Garnishes

Avocado slices

Bacon, crumbled

Banana leaf

Basil leaves, whole or diced

Bell pepper strips

Berries, whole, sliced, or dried

Breadsticks

Broccoli florets

Capers

Cauliflower florets

Caviar

Chili peppers, whole

Chives, whole or diced

Coconut, shredded

Cooked shrimp, whole or diced

Croutons

Cucumber slices

Dill

Edible flowers

Feta cheese, crumbled

Fruit coulis

Hardboiled egg slices

Green beans, whole

Julienned jicama, carrots, turnips

Kiwi slices

Lettuce bed

Melon slices

Mint leaves

Olives

Paprika

Parmesan cheese, grated

Parsley

Pickles, whole or sliced

Pineapple chunks

Salmon roe

Scallions, whole or diced

Seaweed, dry, wet, or whole

Sour cream dollop

Tarragon, whole or diced

Tortilla strips

Whipped cream, dollop

Zucchini strips

Drink Garnishes

Berries, whole or sliced

Celery stalks

Lemon slices or rinds

Lime slices or rinds

Maraschino cherries

Melon chunks

Mint leaves

Olives

Orange slices or rinds

Pearl onions

Pineapple chunks

INGREDIENTS

Newsflash: there is no substitute for quality ingredients! Getting the right food for the right person is as essential to your game as oxygen is to breathing. Shop for ingredients that take your meal from good to "forget dessert, let's bang!" You can't build a home without a foundation. Don't build your den of iniquity without solid materials. It will collapse under the weight of your unbridled lust.

You improve the taste of the meal, your health, and your game. Only unfortunate souls born without taste buds can't tell when they are served crappy food. Your date can tell when you serve the catch of the day or the catch of last month. Don't sell yourself or your libido short. Splurge on the good stuff and you will reap the randy rewards. It'll still be miles cheaper than a trip to Bleu Balls Bistro. Here's a little guide of what to buy where and why.

Produce

The best place to acquire produce is at a farmers' market. Whole Foods or your local health food store are good alternatives. Organic produce is always the way to go. The taste, appearance, smell, and health benefits are clear. The problem is organic produce is expensive. The average consumer can't afford to spend four dollars on a perfect tomato. Corporate farming is a grim reality of the Western world. The pesticides and growth hormones are in everything we consume. But it is worth trying to negotiate better prices at the farmers' market; appeal to the hippie in them. Should that fail, decide how important said ingredient is to your recipe. And if you're making an heirloom tomato salad, just auction off one of your unborn children.

Cheese

There is cheese and then there is CHEESE. Getting *cheese* to make a pizza, quesadilla, or to throw on top of a burrito is easy as picking up a three-pack of Trojans at the gas station. But CHEESE is the glorious by-product of milk from animals such as cows, goats, and sheep. It belongs on gorgeous platters accompanied by crackers, apple slices, dried figs, salami, and bread. I'm talking Humboldt Fog, sharp Irish Cheddar, Roquefort, blue, Burrata, and my favorite, Brie. CHEESE can be found in the specialty cheese section of your local supermarket. It may seem pretentious, but try going to a cheese shop where you can order small slivers of a variety of cheeses. Your libido and taste buds will agree that it was worth the expense.

Meat

When I say meat, I'm not talking about your junk. I'm talking about the carnage of dead animals we slaughter because they taste so bloody good. Getting the freshest cuts of meat is important, though not as essential as when buying seafood. You can get away with picking up meat from the supermarket butcher, wrapped up in cellophane or frozen like Han Solo. But specialized cuts of meat like filet mignon and Kobe beef should be bought from a specialty butcher. Lucky for you amateurs, only a true foodie can distinguish good cuts of beef from the premium shit.

Seafood

I am a seafood whore. Ever see a guy turning tricks in the alley behind a sushi joint? That's probably me. I ain't ashamed to admit the taste, health benefits, and aphrodisiacal qualities get me hard. Still, you gotta have standards. Seafood should be top shelf or don't bother. If you have the means monetarily and geographically, go to a proper fish market, or fishmonger (Shakespearean for "fish pimp"). Accept no substitutes for sashimi-grade fish during your adventures with uncooked fish. If you must, go to your supermarket seafood department but never buy or eat anything that smells fishy. Food poisoning is as sexy as a Queen Elizabeth strip tease.

Exotic Ingredients

Set me loose in an Asian market and watch me fill up three shopping carts with exotic ingredients I have no clue how to pronounce. Asian, Latin, Caribbean, African, and Middle Eastern stores are often the only place to find random ingredients from far, far away. You can get creative in the kitchen by substituting for an exotic ingredient with something available in a regular supermarket, but you are depriving yourself a world-class culinary education. The bodega down the street from my house has obscenely cheap produce and meat for a third of the price in the white man's supermarket. Some supermarkets have a small ethnic food section, but these items are priced exorbitantly and of questionable quality. The Internet isn't just for porn; you can use it to find competitively priced exotic food items. Now take your date to the distant land between the sheets!

DATE'S PREFERENCES

You best serve yourself when you serve your date what they like. Nothing will turn off your date quicker than triggering their gag reflex. Save that for banging. During a blind taste test, Nobel Prize–winning scientists fed two female test subjects different foods. The test subject that got sashimi banged the nerdy scientist on the spot; they're stilling scraping the remnants of the scientist off the wall who fed his test subject cat food.

It may not be the entire dish; often it is one ingredient that people find unpalatable to the point of violent retching. It may be a flavor; it may be the texture; it may be psychosomatic. These tastes often stem from some childhood trauma related to food. Just accept it. Some people's eating preferences make less sense than lapdogs as pets. I have a friend who won't eat herbs. Herbs! The foundation of flavor. But this same friend eats chicken feet by the bucket full. Ridiculous yes. Gross certainly. But that's her bag.

No doubt, your dates will have their own eating preferences. That is why doing your research is worth every ounce of effort. As stated in the last chapter, snoop around to find out what ingredients open the doors and avoid the ones that close them. Never serve someone a meal they view as a lesser alternative to eating stale roadkill.

Pay attention to what they say, write, or infer. It pays off in decadent dividends. If they mention how much they loved their Thailand vacation, make some pad thai. If beets are their favorite vegetable, whip up a Beet (Your Meat) Salad (page 69). Your date will misconstrue you as a thoughtful individual with impeccable taste. This will help build toward the connection you can exploit to bang.

DIETARY RESTRICTIONS

There are dietary restrictions of any fathomable kind. Some are legitimate and scientifically sound. Others are spiritual and based on ancient beliefs that defy logic. Some are intended to make the eater healthier. Others are just pretentious and annoying. My advice is to adapt to bang. Blow off these restrictions and your game will come to a screeching halt. You must acquiesce, not molest!

Religious Restrictions

Some religions forbid eating pork. Others say beef is sacred. Some declare shellfish evil. Many forbid you to drink alcohol. My religion states that if I abstain from sex, I will spend eternity crouched in the back of a station wagon discussing purity with the Jonas Brothers. You must adapt to these restrictions to manipulate your way into this superstitious lot's pants. This will be a challenge if your date is devout. They likely subscribe to the edict of no premarital sexual relations. Even a Cook to Bang master chef may not be able to break the iron will of a zealot. That doesn't mean we won't try!

Health Restrictions

Health restrictions must be respected. *Cook to Bang* encourages you to manipulate your dates, but not at the cost of their health. Some people are cursed with the inability to enjoy the simple pleasures derived from food. This is a shame. I know many lactose-intolerant people who can't comprehend the joy of ice cream brain freeze. Some can't eat wheat products, so a simple sandwich is beyond their scope. Others cannot eat protein or they risk brain damage. All of these are legitimate excuses for not eating the feast you slaved over a hot stove to create. Don't take it personally. Instead, get creative. Demonstrate sensitivity to their needs and they will see to yours.

Vegetarians, Vegans, and Raw Foodists

I was once a vegetarian. I even tried going vegan for a week. But my love for pizza and sushi was too strong. Denying culinary pleasures is beyond me. But there are plenty of amazing meals that do not require meat, dairy, or being cooked at all. These meals are healthier and make brain synapses fire just fine. Sure your palette may shrink servicing the demands of a crazy person. But I am all for the challenge so long as my date is not preachy or annoying. The problem with these dietary restrictions is that they are antisocial and alienate the cook. Ask my mother, who refused to ever serve my vegan friend food again after he physically picked apart her culinary masterpiece. Raw foodists are annoyingly high maintenance and are usually balancing out their toxic life with their peculiar diet. Just slip them a different slab of meat after dinner.

Fad Diets

Nothing drives me batty like someone marching like a zombie to the tune of the latest fad diet: Atkins, South Beach, The Zone, Lemonade, Cabbage, and the Lobotomy Diet are idiotic alternatives to a balanced diet and exercise. Crackpots and pseudo-doctors invent these complicated schemes with nonsensical rules that require exorbitant amounts of money to participate. They are cults, not unlike Scientology or the Moonies. Oftentimes these diets are harmful to one's health. No diet that says you can eat steak by the kilo and drink milkshakes can be good for you. But Cook to Bang chefs should know that zombies subscribing to these systems have low self-esteem and will bang you on the first date. So just play along!

HEALTHY FOOD = SEXY FOOD

The sexiest foods happen to be the healthiest. This is not some bizarre coincidence brought on by two comets colliding three galaxies away a billion years before Jesus rode atop a triceratops. Foods low in fat, high in protein and fiber, and not drowned in oil look prettier and make your body function better. There is a reason why you don't take dates to a sports bar. If you are one of those people, I've reserved some special advice for you:

- Drinking and driving is good for your health
- Safety locks on guns are useless
- Procreation is for losers, condoms are way cool

I don't care if you think deep-fried cheese sticks are phallic. The girl is not going to turn into a sex-crazed nympho in spandex from a White Snake video. Sorry. She'll more likely pass out in a food coma than from a screaming orgasm. Your sports haunt lacks the proper atmosphere to build intimacy, with your buddies hollering at you from across the bar. Wouldn't it be easier to stay home and Cook to Bang?

That cliché "you are what you eat" is more true in today's age of deep-fried Twinkies and funnel cakes. Drink tablespoons of lard and you will be a lard-ass. Serve nutrient-rich food that tastes like an angel wing dipped in wasabi and you will soar. Those who have inevitably banged after a sushi dinner know of what I speak. Many of these super foods are double agent aphrodisiacs. They are that good. More on this in the following chapter. The effects of the sensual kind aren't just superstitious juju. Aphrodisiacs run your body like premium gasoline, so you can fornicate with regularity and stamina. Do you want to run like a Ferrari or a Studebaker?

Shop around the perimeter of the supermarket. Stick to the produce, meat, and seafood. That's where you find the nutrients to gas up your turbo-charged love machine. The aisles are filled with overpriced, processed foods lubed up with hidden calories that leave you limp. Rock the fresh, nutritious ingredients and you will impress your date and cardiologist. Your stock rises when you serve an awesome homemade salad, but flatlines when the microwaved chili cheeseburger pops out. I love crappy food, too, just not when I'm Cooking to Bang. There will be plenty of time for cardiac arrests when you're trading war stories with your buddies back at the sports bar.

FRESHED *VS*. CANNED *VS*. FROZEN

This is an important issue you need to answer when figuring out your meal. There are some dates you can impress with a steaming can of generic beef chili. But is that the type of person you want to bang? Sounds like a gassy affair. Here is the Cook to Bang take on what you can get away with and what you shouldn't.

Getting Fresh

There are few things more satisfying than fresh-caught fish or fruit right off a tree. (I *can* think of one; it rhymes with *hanging*.) Picture the crispness of lettuce, the creaminess of a ripe avocado, meat so tender it belongs in a Lucite case at the Guggenheim. Eating fresh food isn't reality for many of us. Whole Foods, aka Whole Paycheck, is like a strip club for foodies. Look, but don't touch the merchandise! Spending bundles of cash to eat at home defeats the purpose. Fancy restaurants aren't thawing out their ingredients—or are they? Don't blow your wad at the market, but don't skimp out on the essentials like a great piece of fish or an artichoke. You can find the balance between going broke and looking like a cheap loser that eats cold beans from the can.

Canned Sex Appeal

You can't pour a three-course meal out of a can. But canned food will survive a nuclear holocaust. The zombies will roam the streets hungry for brains, but you will be safe, watching DVDs and eating your metallic feast. Then you can Cook to Bang the lingerie models you're sharing your bomb shelter with.

None of us will be picky about what we eat if the shit goes down. There is a tinfoil lining, though: there are plenty of kick-ass meals that can be made with canned goods. Certain canned goods no Cook to Bang chef can live without: black beans, tomatoes, corn, tuna, coconut milk, and lump crabmeat. Don't let your date see you pouring your "gourmet dinner" out of the can. Play it off that they're all fresh ingredients. You're that good.

Putting It on Ice

Freezing items extends their shelf life. Many fine ingredients are cheaper frozen, like fruit, vegetables, and meat. You risk freezer burn, but this can be an acceptable alternative to rotting food in your fridge. Tortillas and chicken are always good for the Han Solo freeze treatment. Frozen fruit is ideal for smoothies and work great as filling for pies and crumbles. Be warned that nothing will taste as good defrosted as fresh. Microwaves are efficient flavor-killing machines. The solution is to drown the bland taste in as much tasty firepower as you can assemble.

BUDGET TO BANG

How do you get the most bang for your buck? Plan your menu with precision and you will avoid the poorhouse and the whorehouse. Be pragmatic, not spasmodic. How much are you willing to spend on the meal? You should design a menu that services your goals on a budget you can afford. Foie gras and white truffles are tits, but there are plenty of recipes you won't have to rob an old lady to buy. You are Cooking to Bang, not taking your date out for seventy-five-dollar thimbles of dessert wine from the French Alps. You can keep the price low without sacrificing quality control.

Whole Foods won't be your first destination on a generic beer budget. Try shopping at the ethnic markets or cutting out the extravagant ingredients. Cooking vegetarian by default could rack you up some Hippie Harlot brownie points. You won't spend that much, your health will improve, and think about all that exercise from banging! Cooking to Bang on a budget just gives you more room to be creative and blow your date's mind . . . and a few other things.

Grocery shopping can become a game: make something amazing with a teeny, tiny budget. Have a nominal figure in your head for all the food, drinks, and condoms, and then ready, set, go! Just don't go over budget! If the halibut fillets are more than you planned, skip the dried porcini mushrooms and improvise, damnit! Use that magnificent brain of yours and your date will be impressed so long as it doesn't taste like burnt rubber.

KINKY KITCHEN ESSENTIALS

Most young singles' kitchens are barren wastelands of beer cans and pizza boxes. Getting your groove on requires making a good first impression. Sure you can make a mind-blowing meal with a hotplate and stale Cheetos. But why limit yourself when these items are available for cheap at the Good Will or 99¢ Only Store? I have fallen in love with every essential kitchen utensil at some point. My kitchen companions have been there for me when nary a woman was in sight. So allow me this moment to serenade these old lovers of mine.

SHARP KNIFE: Who's the sharpest cat that cuts through all the grub? Knife! You damn right. Who's the wing(wo)man that could protect you from another man? Knife! Right on.

SERRATED KNIFE: So what if you aren't "the sharpest knife in the drawer"? It's always a happy ending when you slice and dice my tomatoes and breadbasket.

NONSTICK FRYING PAN: I manhandle you daily and you never nag or get clingy. My mornings wouldn't be the same if I couldn't crack my huevos on your face.

STOCKPOT: Ooh baby, you warm my bones come wintertime. Thinking about the countless nights we spent together boiling and steaming makes me souper crazy.

SPATULA: Flip it, press it, serve that shit up. Ignore my date's cold stare. She's just jealous because I take my time with you.

WOODEN STIRRING SPOON: You give me wood and never fuck up my pan's chi. Oooommmooohhhyyyeeeaaahhh!

STOVE: You heat my life up like a gas explosion inside my heart. A night without you is like a night without condoms and Al Green. Keep broiling!

TOASTER OVEN: I finally met my perfect match for quickies. You make finger food foreplay as hassle free as hiring a mute hooker.

CUTTING BOARD: Thanks for keeping my kitchen looking respectable rather than like the inside of a serial killer's clown car. Now lay down because I'm laying cheese all over you.

SERVING PLATTER: Behold, my trophy wife! You're that sweet, sweet arm candy that impresses my peers, colleagues, and future dates hip to my vibe.

MATCHING DINNER PLATES: Twins! You girls look so fly together. I'd look like a raging jackass if I only had one of you.

WINEGLASSES: Much props to my wingwomen for more sexcapades than I can count on my fingers, toes, and hair follicles. Here's to getting wet and making me look classier than San Diego.

CASSEROLE DISH: You are so deep, girl! You satisfy my every baking need. Fish, chicken, lasagna, dessert! Marinating my seductions since 2003.

MIXING BOWL: We know who mixes it up when shit gets boring. You're always down to toss my salad, salsa dance, and bamboozle some booze.

TINFOIL: You're my sexy spaceman adventure time companion. Now it's time to make shiny recyclable underwear while keeping my pans clean, leftovers fresh, and breakfast burritos hot in the car.

BBQ GRILL: Men love getting up in your grill. I like to think our relationship is based on a mutual love of fire. Pyromania, nymphomania, these are two words that mean the same thing.

CHEESE GRATER: Holla at my bisexual porn star that goes any which way! You'll grate cheese, but you're down to go AC/DC on some veggies. Just let me watch. Cool?

HANDHELD BLENDER: *BUZZZZZZZ!* That's the sound of you giving more pleasure than an industrial-strength vibrator. You blend, chop, and puree with no messy splooge from the blender. Is there any need you don't satisfy?

5

Aphrodisiacs
Anonymous

My name is Spencer and I am an addict. I am addicted to aphrodisiacs. It took me a long time to accept this. After countless mornings waking up next to a naked woman I barely knew, I realized I had to take control. Aphrodisiacs have taken over my life. They sneak into everything I cook. The demon inside me demands I feed it. I want to tell it no, but we both know who's in charge. I am the aphrodisiac demon's bitch. Thus I feed it or suffer its wrath.

The results of losing my will and self-control have been extreme. I look better, feel better, and bang better. The food I eat excites me more, which takes my mind off the more sober aspects of life, like taxes. Worse by far is how evil aphrodisiacs make me promiscuous. Foul temptresses are only too keen to lure me into their bed of iniquity where I am forced to perform carnal acts of unimaginable pleasure. As I write this, I am hiding out in the dark, curtains drawn, scribbling by candlelight. Hard-body zombies surround my house. They cry out in ungodly moans for my food and body. These wicked women have no interest in my hopes, dreams, or personality.

To whoever finds this manuscript, the aphrodisiacs got the

best of me. I surely died a sex slave to a harem that forces me to cook and bang them. Please tell my family that I love them. But I have no regrets. I accept that this aphrodisiac outbreak is in many ways my fault. How could I have known that my writings would ruin more lives than crack cocaine and reality television combined? No doubt history will remember me as some perverse pusher-man turning the world on to my addictive products: the Pablo Escobar of the kitchen. With that harsh condemnation in mind, below are my delicious vices. May God have mercy on my soul.

ARTICHOKES = HEROIN

Feel that spike? It's not a hypodermic needle. It's the gentle sting of a spiky artichoke leaf. You won't mind. You are getting your artichoke fix, or as the kids call it, "getting 'choked." On first bite, you feel a surge of sexual power rushing through your body. You feel invincible. No one you share an artichoke with can resist you. But can you resist the 'choke? An artichoke addiction ain't cheap. You will justify it, claiming the nutrients will clean your liver and freshen your breath. Face it: you're a 'choke junkie. Don't be surprised if you wake up with a bowl of used artichoke leaves on your left and a naked play pal on your right.

Don't Artichoke Your Chicken

Why settle for strangling your innocent bird when you can be out there getting someone else to choke it for you? Take the high road with this unadulterated aphrodisiac A-bomb. You are eating a 98.5% payload of vitamins, minerals, and phytochemicals to fuel the evening's cardiovascular requirements. The sexy time explosion spicy aioli will give you a head start in the hot and sweaty department. Happy munching.

> **Total time: approximately 45 minutes**
> **Projected cost: $6**
> **Drinking wingman: Chardonnay, Syrah, or lager**
> **Ingredients:**
>> 1 large artichoke
>> ½ dried chipotle chile, finely chopped
>> 1 clove garlic, finely chopped
>> 1 lemon, halved
>> ½ teaspoon salt
>> 1 teaspoon cayenne pepper
>> 1 tablespoon mayonnaise

Steam the artichoke over high heat until it opens up and you can pull out the leaves with ease, 35 to 45 minutes. Make the aioli while the artichoke steams.

Mix together the chipotle, garlic, juice from ½ the lemon, salt, and cayenne pepper with the mayonnaise. Refrigerate until the artichoke and your date are ready to rumble.

Cut the steamed artichoke down the middle slowly. Scoop out the wispy flowery center with a spoon, leaving the artichoke's bigger leaves and heart (aka G-spot) intact. Squeeze the remaining lemon half over the artichoke halves and serve them on a plate with the aioli.

ASPARAGUS = SPANISH FLY

Asparagus spears aren't sharp enough to kill a water buffalo, but they can pierce your date's heart—and shatter any resistance they may have. Seventeenth-century UK naturalist Nicholas Culpepper hailed asparagus for "stirring up lust in man and woman." Spanish fly is used to make farm animals breed; asparagus makes humans bang like farm animals. This mysterious vegetable is loaded with potassium and vitamin A, which boost sex drives and folic acid, which produces histamines that rev up the power of an orgasm. The fact that asparagus makes your pee smell weird is a bonus.

Tap That Ass-paragus Soup

Soup's sex appeal is underestimated because most people conjure up the canned shit. If history, health, and sex aren't motivating factors, consider that homemade soup tastes bloody amazing. The extra-aphrodisiac boost of crab in this recipe will keep it going on 'til the break of dawn.

Total time: approximately 40 minutes
Projected cost: $13
Drinking wingman: Merlot or Riesling
Ingredients:
> 1 onion, coarsely chopped
> 1 tablespoon olive oil
> 1 pound asparagus, coarsely chopped
> ½ lemon
> 2 cups chicken broth
> ½ cup plain yogurt
> 6 ounces lump crabmeat
> ½ teaspoon salt
> Black pepper, to taste

Sauté the onion in a stockpot with the oil over medium heat until the onion becomes translucent, about 2 minutes. Add the asparagus and cook until they soften like your date's heart, about 3 minutes.

Squeeze in the juice from the lemon. Add the broth and bring it to a roaring boil over high heat. Then turn the heat to low and simmer, covered, for 20 minutes. Make a subtle move, perhaps a warm embrace, or nibble on their ear while you wait.

Turn off the heat when the asparagus bleeds green into the stock and the veggies are softened. Pour in the yogurt and puree the concoction in a blender or with your trusty hand-held blender. Mix in the crab with a spoon, but do not puree! Add salt and pepper to taste. Serve in bowls. Let the soup work its magic and then the real magic begins.

AVOCADO = MARIJUANA

Dude, this avocado is the awesomest shit, bro. It like totally makes every meal, like . . . better. You know?

Avocado is soft, green, and creamy with the good fat. You'll get the munchies to chomp down on whatever it is served with. All that organic fiber, folate, vitamins B_6, C, and E, beta-Sitosterol, and glutathione open up your chakras to this ancient Aztec sex stimulant. Be the shaman and throw a little of this green love machine on your salad and sandwiches to up the sex appeal. Be careful, avocado is a gateway food that could lead to harder aphrodisiacs.

Stiffly Stuffed Avocado

Straight out of a schmancy country club comes this stuffed avocado, turbo-loaded with aphrodisiacs. The avocado works wonders for your libido, but combine it with chili and shrimp and you have *The Guns of Navarone* firing out your mouth and down south. It's simultaneously sweet, tangy, spicy, and creamy, like a lover who's a meek librarian by day and bisexual S&M stripper by night.

Total time: approximately 5 minutes

Projected cost: $8

Drinking wingman: Arnold Palmer . . . with vodka if you're feeling it

Ingredients:

> ¼ pound cooked shrimp, tails removed
> 1 hardboiled egg
> ¼ red onion, finely chopped
> 1 radish, finely chopped
> 1 stalk celery, finely chopped
> 1 jalapeño or serrano chile, finely chopped
> ½ red bell pepper, finely chopped
> ½ lime
> 1 tablespoon mayonnaise
> 1 avocado, split lengthwise
> Salt, to taste
> 2 handfuls shredded lettuce

Slice the shrimp down the middle. Chop up the hardboiled egg. Mix together the shrimp, chopped egg, onion, radish, celery, chile, and bell pepper. Squeeze ¼ of the lime juice into the mixture and add the mayonnaise.

Scoop the avocado meat intact from their shells (use spoon for best results). Discard the pit and shells like a used condom. Overstuff the shrimp mixture into each avocado half's indentation. Squeeze the remaining lime juice over the avocados and add salt, if you like. Serve it up over a bed of lettuce.

BASIL = LIPITOR

Basil and Lipitor are the most used items in their respective fields: herbs and pharmaceuticals. This love leaf aids circulation and increases women's sex drives and fertility. It's all about this *it* herb whose scent is fabled to drive men like me crazy. My basil plant died and I nearly croaked from withdrawal. The fact that basil tastes so damn good is almost beside the point.

Pesto Bango! Chicken Sinwich

POOF! That's the sound of clothes disappearing. Just ask the art chick I invited over for some post-gallery nosh. She took one bite of my green sandwich and her top vanished. She wasn't even done with the first half when her skirt imploded. The ability to make clothing disappear, a goal that baffled nerdy scientists for centuries, has now been achieved with the enchanted aphrodisiacal pesto. MAGIC 1–SCIENCE 0

Total time: approximately 10 minutes
Projected cost: $10
Drinking wingman: Slutty Temple (page 108)
Ingredients:
    1 large chicken breast

2 tablespoons pesto*
1 tablespoon olive oil
2 sandwich rolls
Mayonnaise, spread at your discretion
1 tomato, thinly sliced
½ avocado, sliced

Flatten the chicken breast with a mallet or your fists of fury. Spread 1 tablespoon of the pesto on one side of the chicken. Heat the oil in a pan over medium heat and cook the chicken pesto side down. Spread the remaining pesto on the top of the chicken. Cook through, flipping once using spatula to keep pesto crust intact, about 3 minutes per side. Cut the tasty green meat in half.

Split the bread rolls, leaving one edge intact. Spread mayonnaise, or condom-ment of your choice, over the bread and stuff it with the pesto chicken, tomatoes, and avocado. Close up shop, slice it in half, and watch clothing mysteriously vanish.

BEETS = STEROIDS

Don't make me beet your ass! Sorry, it's just the beet-roid rage. The high boron content is pumping my blood up. Beets make men stronger, faster, better athletes and lovers without shrinking their junk or giving them steroid bitch tits. Dudes can OD on beets and still play baseball without a bra. You'll be well equipped to "take favors in the beetroot fields," an early twentieth century euphemism for visiting prostitutes.

---

* Chop or blend 4 parts fresh basil to 1 part each of Parmesan cheese, olive oil, pine nuts, and garlic. Your lazy ass can just buy a jar, but that's not as classy!

Beet (Your Meat) Salad

Beets and goat cheese form a union on par with Sonny and Cher, *or* condoms and lube, *or* Sonny and Cher using condoms and lube. They are your friends and allies when it comes to motivating hanky panky. Beet salad is a classy choice for a first date because it's neither expensive nor expected. It's refreshing, invigorating, and will cue you up a night not beating your meat.

Total time: approximately 10 minutes
Projected cost: $10
Drinking wingman: Cabernet or Chardonnay
Ingredients:
    2 beets, stalks removed
    1 pear
    1 (8-ounce) log goat cheese
    Balsamic vinegar, to taste
    Olive oil, to taste

Steam or boil the beets until they can easily be stabbed through with a fork. Throw the beets into a container filled with ice-cold water and allow them to cool in the fridge, approximately 30 minutes. The skins will then easily peel off. Cut the beets into 1-inch-thick rounds. Core the pear and then cut lengthwise into ½-inch thick slices. Cut the goat cheese into ½-inch rounds.

Create stacks of the holy trinity, sandwiching the goat cheese between beet and pear slices. Drizzle the vinegar and oil over them and serve. Two or 3 stacks per plate make a spectacular starter or a healthy lunch before an afternoon quickie.

BLACK BEANS = XANAX

Experiencing anxiety or stress? Are you depressed or on the verge of a panic attack? Put down that pill bottle and stuff some black beans in your mouth hole. It's a socially acceptable habit that you can indulge in public without scorn. These high-grade beans have enough protein, fiber, and folic acid to get your heart pumping. Plus the tryptophan will ease you both into the mood for humping.

Huevos Grandes Rancheros

This breakfast dish's sustenance can satisfy the macho tough guy and seduce the daintiest of conquests. We're talking *desayuno* loaded with black bean aphrodisiac goodness and egg protein power and veggie delights. You'll be coming for years to come. I prepared this meal for a señorita that was surprised a gringo could make huevos rancheros. They were nearly as tasty as the love siesta we took after breakfast.

Total time: approximately 20 minutes
Projected cost: $4
Drinking wingman: Not-So-Teeny-Weeny Bellini (page 105)
Ingredients:
   1 small onion, coarsely chopped
   2 tablespoons olive oil
   1 handful cilantro, chopped
   1½ tomatoes, roughly chopped
   1 (16-ounce) can black beans
   2 eggs
   2 corn tortillas
   Salsa
   ½ avocado, thinly sliced

Sauté the onions with 1 tablespoon of the oil in a pan over medium heat for approximately 2 minutes. Throw in the cilantro, tomatoes and beans and simmer together, covered, for approximately 10 minutes.

Uncover the pan and crack each egg gently over the simmering ranchero sauce mixture. Cover the pan again and poach the eggs until they go white, but before yolks harden, approximately 5 minutes. Remove the poached eggs from the sauce with a slotted spoon or spatula and set aside.

Heat the remaining oil in a small pan over medium heat. Warm each tortilla separately so it browns, rises, and then flattens out, approximately ten seconds. Place the tortillas on plates and divide the ranchero sauce evenly between them. Add the eggs and crown them with salsa and avocado slices.

CHILES = ECSTASY

Spicy chiles make you techno dance party all night long! It's like seasoning your food with E. Even the most mundane meal is given a danceable beat without you losing brain cells or poisoning your spinal fluid. Chiles also open up your pleasure receptors and release endorphins, energizing you so you feel like you're floating. Your heart rate will rise, you'll sweat, get chills, even blurred vision when you've got the good stuff. Familiar sensation, no? Embrace it, along with your date, and feel the vibe.

5 (Orgasm) Alarm Veggie Chili

Veggie chili is healthy, tasty, and bangable. I once made this dish for a Super Bowl party rumored to be packed with hotties. It was a struggle not to finish off this aphrodisiac addict's wet dream before the party. I controlled my cravings long enough to blow everyone's mind and collect a few phone numbers.

I snuck away at halftime with the leftovers and indulged my-self in the dark with a spoon and a smile.

Total time: approximately 45 minutes
Projected cost: $8
Drinking wingman: Panty-Dropping Shandy (page 106)
Ingredients:

> 4 cloves garlic, finely chopped
> ½ cup vegetable oil
> 1 onion, coarsely chopped
> 1 large carrot, chopped
> 2 celery stalks, coarsely chopped
> 3 bell peppers (red, yellow, green), coarsely chopped
> 2 dried New Mexico chiles, chopped
> 2 handfuls chopped white button mushrooms
> 2 tablespoons ground cumin
> 1 tablespoon dried oregano
> 1 teaspoon salt
> 1 (28-ounce) can whole tomatoes, with juice
> 1 (16-ounce) can corn
> 1 (28-ounce) can garbanzo beans
> 1 (16-ounce) can black beans
> Shredded Cheddar cheese, for garnish
> Sour cream, for garnish
> ½ red onion, finely diced, for garnish

Sauté the garlic with the vegetable oil over medium-high in a stockpot until they brown, approximately 30 seconds. Sauté the onions until they become translucent, approximately 2 min-utes. Add the carrots, celery, and bell peppers and cook until they soften, approximately 15 minutes.

Get the spicy train going and add the New Mexico chiles. Toss in the mushrooms and simmer, approximately 2 minutes. Now smack it all up with the cumin, oregano, and salt and cook in the flavor, approximately 10 minutes.

Coarsely chop up the canned tomatoes and add them with their juice to the pot. Cook until the tomatoes dissolve and become part of the sauce, approximately 10 minutes.

Drain the liquid from the corn, garbanzo, and black beans. Dump them into the pot and cook until everything becomes united in chili power, approximately 10 minutes. Serve it up in bowls garnished with Cheddar, sour cream, and red onion.

CHOCOLATE = CRACK

Few things hook you quicker than your first hit of chocolate. It courses through your bloodstream and creates an intense euphoria and sense of well-being. Chocolate can make men explosive in the sack and unleash a woman's inhibited sexy beast. You will spend the rest of your days chasing that first chocolate high. Turn your date into your crack ho. Just don't become that choc-head who robs a Godiva store.

Pinch-Your-Ass-Berry Brownies

This dish is so sensual I seduced myself and totally forgot my date was there. She couldn't keep her finger out of my batter and licked my bowls clean! We nearly polished the batter off before it even made it into the oven. These brownies are radioactive with awesomeness. This is what dessert in heaven will taste like, minus the annoying harp music. Accept the raspberry brownies into your heart and sing a postcoital Hallelujah!

Total time: approximately 15 minutes

Projected cost: $14

Drinking wingman: Smoking Hot Peppermint Fatty
    (pages 108–109) or Naughty Eggnog (pages 104–105)

Ingredients:

> 2/3 cup baking flour
> 3/4 cup sweetened cocoa powder
> 3/4 cup sugar
> 1/4 teaspoon salt
> 1/4 teaspoon baking powder
> 1 stick unsalted butter (1/2 cup)
> 2 eggs
> 1 teaspoon vanilla extract
> 1 cup semisweet chocolate chips
> 1/2 pack fresh or frozen raspberries

Preheat the oven to 350°F. Sift together the flour, cocoa, sugar, salt, and baking powder. Melt the butter over low heat in a small saucepan or pot. Beat in the eggs and vanilla extract. Add the egg-butter mixture to the cocoa mixture and mix together to form a batter. Blend in the chocolate chips. You now have a mind-blowing batter to bake or lick off your date.

Grease a small baking pan. Pour in half the batter like a pleasure-delaying seduction. Tuck those bang-a-licious berries into the brownie batter bed before smothering it with the rest of the cocoa-laden chaos. Bake until you can dip a toothpick into the brownies and it comes out dry, 35 to 45 minutes. Allow them to cool for approximately 15 minutes and serve with ice cream, a glass of milk, or your smoothest closing move.

FIGS = HASHISH

Figs are Bible-famed aphrodisiac fixes that look like a woman's unmentionables. Adam and Eve were munching on figs in the Garden of Eden before Eve put the wrong thing in her mouth. She knew it was illegal, but she ate the forbidden fruit anyway! Like hashish, figs are uncommon in the States so it's a rarified treat to indulge in. The aphrodisiac flavonoids, polyphenols, and antioxidants are concentrated, so they put you in a euphoric haze and keep you banging long and strong.

Quesa-diddle-ya

Just when your toaster oven thought it was safe from your simple seductions, here comes a kinky quesadilla. Buying the ingredients should be the toughest part. Figs can be pricey, but they are aphrodisiacs of biblical proportions. Isn't a night of unspeakable acts worth the cost? These quesadillas also make great appetizers to preassemble and take to a backyard BBQ or a Super Bowl or keys-in-the-punchbowl party.

Total time: approximately 10 minutes
Projected cost: $6
Drinking wingman: Panty-Dropping Shandy (page 106)
Ingredients:
    1 handful chopped figs or 1 tablespoon fig jam
    1 medium tortilla
    4 thin slices Brie

1 handful crushed candied walnuts
2 tablespoons mango salsa
½ avocado, thinly sliced

Spread the fig jam evenly over half the tortilla. Place Brie slices and candied walnuts on the other half. Close the tortilla.

Throw it in toaster oven and cook until toasted. Or fry it in an oiled pan until each side is browned. Cut into four pieces and serve with sliced avocado and mango salsa.

GINGER = VIAGRA

Bob Dole and his little blue pill ain't got shit on the big brown root. Ginger has been pumping blood into men's willies since they wrote the Kama Sutra. Its badass scent alone can get a man's heart rate up and make him sweat like he's already banging. Erectile dysfunction has been trumped by nature's erotic touch. No shame in OD'ing on ginger because it's for your date's benefit. Should a ginger-fueled erection last more than four hours, don't contact a physician. Call another date for a late-night snack.

Naughty Mahi

There are a lot of slutty fish, but no fish is as whorish as mahi mahi. This dolphinfish takes after its sex-crazed mammal namesake. Rub the mahi mahi down with sweet ginger love and the fish will tap your ass on the ocean floor. It will never call you again, but who cares? The mahi mahi's aphrodisiacal slut factor, when accompanied by sautéed veggies, papaya salsa, and avocado, will leave your date powerless to your naughtiest whims. Come to think of it, you better make enough food for three . . .

Total time: approximately 15 minutes
Projected cost: $14
Drinking wingman: Sauvignon Blanc or Bangria (pages 100–101)
Ingredients:
   2 (8-ounce) mahi mahi fillets
   2 tablespoons diced fresh ginger
   ½ lime
   2 tablespoons olive oil
   1 teaspoon salt
   ½ teaspoon black pepper
   1 onion, cut into long, thin strips
   1 red bell pepper, cut into long, thin strips
   1 tomato, coarsely chopped
   2 tablespoons papaya salsa
   ½ avocado, thinly sliced

Marinate the mahi mahi fillets with the ginger, the juice from the lime, 1 tablespoon of the oil, salt, and black pepper, for approximately 10 minutes.

Sauté the onions and bell peppers in the remaining oil for approximately 3 minutes. Add the tomato and cook until softened and then stew approximately 4 minutes. Lay out a veggie bed on each plate.

Sauté or grill the mahi mahi until the fish whitens and browns a little, flipping once, approximately 2 minutes per side. Serve the fillets over the veggie bed and crown each with a tablespoon of papaya salsa and a slice of avocado. I think I just got a little wet.

HONEY = BOOZE

I have drunk more than one jarful of honey thinking it was just a sweet, perfect cocktail. Like a bender at a tranny strip joint, my honey binges always end with me feeling sticky and confused. I discover later the insane shit I've done under the influence of bee's brew. You can't blame me though. Honey's rich in vitamin B, the root of testosterone, and boron, which produces estrogen. Both sexes become more up for it once Aphrodite's nectar takes effect. Why do you think they call it a honeymoon?

Forbidden Fruit Salad

This salad is reserved for the harvest gods. Giving you this recipe is akin to Prometheus giving man fire. Sure I'll wash a mountain of dishes for all eternity for my transgression, but helping you get you laid six ways from Sunday makes it all worth it. The Forbidden Fruit Salad always delivers, sexing up countless dull breakfasts and lunches. Did I mention this ultra-healthy salad makes bodily secretions taste better? (No, not your shit, sicko.)

Total time: approximately 25 minutes
Projected cost: $7
Drinking wingman: Raging Hard (On) Lemonade (pages 106–107)
Ingredients:
    1 cup water

½ lemon

1 small handful whole cloves

1 teaspoon ground cinnamon

2 tablespoons honey

1 banana, thinly sliced

1 tangerine, sectioned

3 kiwis, peeled and cut into eighths

1 mango, cut into bite-size pieces

Boil the water. Zest the lemon half and toss in the zest along with the cloves, cinnamon, and honey. Simmer until the honey absorbs the flavors, approximately 10 minutes.

Strain out the spice debris from the honey mixture and squeeze in the juice from the zested lemon half. Allow mixture to cool for approximately 10 minutes before tossing it with the pornocopia of fruit. Serve up the fruit salad confident that you could fight off any cold or cold streak.

OYSTERS = LEVITRA

If ginger is the Viagra of aphrodisiacs, then oysters are the more potent Levitra. These slippery bounties of the sea rev up male potency with off-the-chart zinc levels. And if that's not enough of a reason to shuck oyster shells, consider the D-aspartic acid and NMDA compounds that can trigger hormones like testosterone and estrogen. You may be hoping to find a pearl in an oyster, but I'm sure you'll settle for a pearl necklace.

Oysters Rockefella Skank

Just because you're not a Rockefeller doesn't mean you can't eat like one. Besides, all the fancy cars and diamond-encrusted

Rolexes are just a means to get gold-digging skanks to bang you. So make like a goddamn Rockefeller and indulge in the rich oyster power. The aphrodisiac supernovas of the sea will rev up your loins like a golf cart run on plutonium. You'll feel momentarily like the richest dude on the planet slurping these suckers down.

Total time: approximately 20 minutes
Projected cost: $15
Drinking wingman: Champagne
Ingredients:
 2 tablespoons unsalted butter
 1 strip bacon, finely chopped
 1/2 tablespoon minced fresh ginger
 1 tablespoon finely chopped spinach
 1 tablespoon minced onion
 1 tablespoon finely chopped fresh parsley
 2 tablespoons breadcrumbs
 1/2 teaspoon salt
 1/4 lemon
 12 raw oysters, shucked (your fish pimp can do this for you)

Preheat the oven to broil. Create the filling by melting butter on low heat. Add the bacon, ginger, spinach, onion, parsley, breadcrumbs, salt, and the juice from the lemon and cook through, approximately 10 minutes.

Top each oyster with a small scoop of the filling. Broil them until the topping is browned, approximately 5 minutes. Serve them up with lemon slices or your favorite hot sauce.

APHRODISIAC OVERDOSE—A CAUTIONARY TALE

During a Mardi Gras college trip, I gorged at an all-you-can-eat New Orleans oyster bar. The aphrodisiac power of oysters and chiles (Tabasco sauce) kicked in right when my girlfriend passed out drunk. She was on the rag and unsympathetic to my raging libido. I was forced to rub myself raw watching hotel porn on mute. And I was still hard as rock the entire next day. Consider yourself forewarned.

PINE NUTS = LOVE POTION NO. 9

Skeptics say "Love Potion No. 9" is just a cheesy 50s doo-wop song. Those cranky bitches haven't tried my serum made from the extracted zinc of pine nuts. Similar potions were made during medieval times to get long-married couples banging again. That was before modern chemistry. My shit is so potent, the opposite sex will fall for you *Romeo and Juliet* style. You'll know I've been there first by the trail of pine nuts leading to the bedroom.

Friction Chicken Salad

Friction ain't always a bad thing. It's chemistry and physics at its best. Without body parts commingling in a battle of wills and urges, full release is as likely as a eunuch's stunt-cock porn career. The same rules apply to pine nuts on your libido. Load these gifts from the love gods into your seemingly innocent chicken salad and watch Betty Crocker go Betty Page on your ass.

Total time: approximately 20 minutes
Projected cost: $9
Drinking wingman: Chardonnay or Raging Hard (On)
 Lemonade (pages 106–107)

Ingredients:

- 1/2 pound chicken breast
- 1/2 lime
- 1 teaspoon black pepper
- 1 Fuji apple, cut into long, thin slices
- 1 avocado, cut into long, thin slices
- 1 green endive, cored and cut into 1/4-inch slivers
- 8 kalamata olives, pitted and coarsely chopped
- 1 handful pine nuts
- 1 tablespoon mayonnaise
- 1 teaspoon red wine vinegar

Marinate the chicken in the juice from the lime and the pepper for approximately 10 minutes. Pan-fry the chicken until it is cooked all the way through, flipping to cook both sides evenly, approximately 5 minutes per side. Cut the chicken into long thin strips.

Throw the apple, avocado, endive, olives, pine nuts, and chicken into a salad bowl. Add the mayonnaise and vinegar and toss it all together. Serve it up and commence with the groping.

ROSEMARY = COCAINE

Blow a big fat rail . . . of rosemary. Seriously, try it. I'll wait.

Did you do it? How was it? Feel like a thousand tiny razorblades slicing up your sinuses? Rosemary isn't meant for snorting, jackass. But do you feel the rush? It's iron, calcium, and vitamin B_6 increasing your blood circulation and sensitivity to touch. You'll lose all control once rosemary triggers your scent memories with experiences of the sexual variety. Rosemary tastes and feels so good that you'll find yourself rubbing it all over your gums and down your pants. Now that I have a rosemary bush growing in my yard, I constantly break Scarface's golden rule: Don't get high on your own supply.

Roasted Chicken Rubdown

Roasting a chicken is a lot like a slow, deliberate seduction: if you rush it, you end up with cold meat and food poisoning. But do it right and you will get laid with the kind of gusto that will leave you satisfied for hours—maybe even days! And you'll have some kick-ass leftovers for sandwiches, salads, or to eat right, ahem, off the bone. This hearty dish earns brownie points for effort and is goddamn delicious. It's mostly prep work, and then you can slide it in the oven, crank on the Barry White, and kick your best living room game.

Total time: approximately 90 minutes
Projected cost: $13
Drinking wingman: Pinot Noir or Sauvignon Blanc
Ingredients:

> 1 whole (4-pound) chicken
>
> 1 onion, coarsely chopped
>
> 2 tablespoons achiote seasoning
>
> 8 potatoes, cut into bite-size pieces

2 cloves garlic, thinly sliced
1 handful plucked rosemary
2 tablespoons olive oil

Preheat oven to 350°F. Stuff the chicken with the onion and rub the achiote into the chicken skin, leaving a few clumps on top.

Place the potatoes all around the chicken in the baking pan. Place the garlic slices and rosemary evenly over the chicken and potatoes. Drizzle the chicken with the oil.

Throw the chicken in the oven and roast for 1 to 1½ hours. Flip the potatoes occasionally so they soak up the juices on the bottom of the pan. The bird is ready to please and not cause disease when you see no pink after poking a skewer into the leg or breast. Carve off sections of the bird and serve it up with the potatoes and some of the roasted onions. If your date doesn't appreciate your effort, kick their ass out and enjoy the bird solo. Don't waste this fine product on some unappreciative coke whore.

ROASTED CHICKEN CHEEKY VARIATIONS

- Squeeze lemon over the chicken halfway through the roast for more tangy umph.
- Stuff breadcrumbs into the chicken if you think Dr. Atkins was a fool.
- Add maple syrup for a sweeter taste. Will also come in handy for culinarylingus!

SEAFOOD = PROZAC

Feeling down? Is your OCD flaring up? Are you on the verge of a panic attack? Grab your rod and catch the Prozac of the sea. Beyond the kick-ass taste, seafood is rich in protein and omega-3 fatty acids. It kicks cancer's ass and combats erectile dysfunction. Eating Poseidon's bounty cheers me up, gives me a sense of well-being, and makes me a nicer person. But withdrawal symptoms can be severe. I went homicidal on a bus full of Navy SEALs after being denied sushi for a month. It wasn't pretty. (Don't worry, my face healed prettier than ever.)

Miso Horny Cod

The Japanese approach everything with perfection in mind from manga to ninjas to oral. Miso cod is no exception. It's a little sweet, a little savory, and 100 percent banging. The tender fish breaks off into scrumptious flakes and is complemented by the steamed bok choy. The flavors battle on your tongue in a perfectly choreographed samurai duel. Your date is sure to love you long time.

Total time: approximately 3 hours (mostly for marinating fish)
Projected cost: $15
Drinking wingman: sake, beer, or a dry white wine
Ingredients:

   ¼ **cup sake***
   ⅓ **cup mirin***
   ¾ **cup white miso paste***
   ½ **cup sugar**
   2 **boned black cod fillets***
   4 **baby bok choy***
   2 **tablespoons soy sauce**
   ½ **lemon**

* **Items available at most Japanese or Asian markets**

Boil the sake and mirin on medium heat for 20 to 30 seconds until the alcohol cooks off. Stir in the miso paste until the chunks dissolve into the liquid. Mix in the sugar until it dissolves. Allow the miso sauce to cool.

Pat the cod fillets dry with a paper towel. Slather up the fillets with the miso sauce and marinate in a bowl covered with plastic wrap for at least 2½ hours.

Preheat the oven to broil. Wipe off the excess marinade and place the fillets in a baking pan. Broil the fish until the tops brown. Remove the pan, preheat oven to 400°F, and bake the fish for 10 to 15 minutes.

While the fish bakes, steam the bok choy until the leaves wilt and turn bright green. Toss the steamed bok choy with the soy sauce and the juice from the lemon before serving.

STRAWBERRIES = PLACEBO

Strawberries are not technically aphrodisiacs, but you could have fooled me. These aphrodisiac sugar pills are like edible valentines. Faith and optimism play a powerful role in curing ailments like blue balls and cold streaks. Dip them in chocolate and you are an official resident of aphrodisiac city. A pile of strawberry stems is an excellent omen, like an empty bottle of wine and pile of condom wrappers.

Balls-amic Strawberries

Try dipping this pair in whipped cream. Dessert is the time when Cook turns into Bang. This dish is healthy, tasty, and quick for the instant-gratification crowd. Do not fear the balsamic vinegar, for it is your friend. The fusion of the powdered sugar, fructose from the berries, and the vinegar is like some mystical alchemy that preps your tongue for more adventures.

Be sure to handfeed these to your date, thus fostering the intimacy you will no doubt exploit for your own perverted gains.

Total time: approximately 2 minutes
Projected cost: $4
Drinking wingman: Champagne, of course
Ingredients:
    1 pint fresh strawberries
    ½ lemon
    2 tablespoons balsamic vinegar
    2 tablespoons powdered sugar

Remove the stems from the strawberries and cut into thin slices. Squeeze the juice from the lemon over the strawberries, followed by the vinegar and sugar. Serve this simple satisfaction on a platter and feed them to your lover(s) while they massage your ego.

WATERMELON = CIALIS

Are you feeling weak-willed? Pathetic? Flaccid? Watermelon is the most effective natural cure for ED, especially the rind. Studies have proven that the citrulline naturally triggers arginine, the chemical in Cialis that gets male pistons pumping. The fact that this refreshing fruit contains the cancer-fighting nutrients lycopene and beta-carotene will be lost on most. Forget that elderly Cialis couple lying in separate bathtubs. You'll be sharing a tub filled with melon juice and waterproof sex toys.

Magic Melons Soup

This summer soup will turbo charge your libido so you can take plenty of prisoners in the bedroom. Think Stockholm syndrome. They'll be stuck on you like barnacles on a freighter ship. Did I mention how refreshing chilled watermelon soup is after an exhausting banging session? Now get yourself to the market so you can blow your date's mind, soul, and pelvis.

Total time: approximately 3½ hours (mostly chilling time)
Projected cost: $13
Drinking wingman: add vodka or gin if you're hard to the core
Ingredients:
>   1 small handful chopped fresh ginger
>   1 lime
>   2 handfuls chopped mint leaves
>   1 tablespoon unsalted butter
>   1 large seedless watermelon
>   2 cups white wine
>   ½ cup sugar
>   1 liter club soda
>   1 handful goat cheese

In a stockpot, sauté the ginger, the juice from half the lime, and half the mint leaves in the butter.

Split watermelon in half and scoop the melon meat into the stockpot. Add the white wine and sugar. Puree everything with a handheld blender, bring to a boil, lower the heat, and simmer until you cook the alcohol out, approximately 10 minutes. Let it chill in the fridge, approximately 3 hours.

Ladle the soup into the watermelon halves. Add club soda and the remaining mint leaves and lime juice. Serve it chilled in bowls, crowning with goat cheese crumbles.

6

Libation Lubrication

Newsflash: drinking helps you get laid. I led a team of crack investigative anthropologists who tested that hypothesis. Full disclosure: we blew our grant on strippers and Courvoisier. But we had convincing pie charts, graphs and a PowerPoint presentation. More interesting than our results about drinking was another discovery: combining food with drinks makes for a supernova of sexuality. Apparently washing down a delicious meal with sumptuous liquids awakens demons with an unquenchable thirst for good loving.

So ease the tension, lower your inhibitions, and drink up!

Clearly alcohol increases the odds that boots will knock all night. The loss of boring inhibitions aside, pairing what you eat with what you drink will determine who you bang. Don't be a Neanderthal and eat a filet mignon with light beer. It's like your boss praising your professionalism while an intern blows you under your desk: it doesn't do either justice. The time spent thinking for a moment about what liquids complement what solids will be credits toward you getting naked later.

This isn't anything new. The art of food and drink pairing goes back to ancient times. If the Mesopotamians could pull it off without electricity, motorized transportation, or hygienic methods of fermentation, surely you can buy the right bottle at the store.

What you drink is just as important as what you eat. The perfect pairing of food and drink can create multiple mouth orgasms. Flavors should complement each other, like drinking a beer while banging doggy-style. Why throw a monkey wrench into your well-executed culinary plans by serving seared tuna salad with whole milk? Clever pairings make the case that sleeping with you won't just put them further into slut category— because you're so goddamn classy. You can also earn amnesty for culinary offenses like burnt chicken or mushy pasta with a stiff, tasty beverage.

Pairings are subjective to each person's palette, just like dating. Some guys like big tits, others tight asses. Some girls like tall dudes, others mustaches. One woman's foie gras is another man's chili cheeseburger. Tastes aren't universal. But there are some general rules we can all agree on. Mess these up and any potential banging points you racked up before are a distant memory. Libation lubrication is often the difference between Cook to Bang and Cook to Wank.

YOU BOOZE, YOU LOSE

We all like to get our drink on. But there's no benefit to drinking yourself into a stupor. You can't articulate and you risk not being able to function when the time comes. Besides, it's predatory and sketchy to get your date so wasted they can't say no. The booze you drink should enhance the evening, not dominate it. A wine buzz can kick ass, but could just as easily make you zonk out before the first kiss. Too much sauce and you'll be heading to the bathroom, not getting head in the bedroom. Drink socially, not excessively.

BEER *VS.* WINE *VS.* BOOZE

Choosing your poison comes down to what you're munching on and personal taste. A NASCAR Nasty might be happy with light beer, but that Yummy Yuppie expects the rare vintage Pinot, and most Club Sluts will just slam back Red Bull vodka kamikazes all night. Beer, wine, and booze all have their charms in the pursuit of banging. There is a time and place for each style of booze to land a sexy bird on your perch. Each offers benefits and drawbacks. Beer is refreshing, but filling. Wine is classy, but expensive. Liquor gets you trashed (both a positive and a negative).

WINE, DINE, AND SIXTY-NINE

Wine is without a doubt the sexiest of all drinks. It ages better than most humans (Demi Moore excepted) and is good for your heart. The variety of flavors, aromas, and textures titillate your senses in oh so many special ways. With wine comes faux wisdom. Wine connoisseurs are pretentious bullshit artists, but it never hurts to talk a good wine game. You can't deny that the aroma can be tantalizing and the taste seductive. Don't be surprised if you get the yearning to fuck the wineglass.

HARD AND FAST RULES OF WINE PAIRING

Balance Food and Wine
Strong food flavors = strong wine;
delicate food flavors = delicate wine.

Match Regionally
Italian food = Italian wine; French food = French wine.

Drink from the Right Glass
There's a reason for specific red, white, and Champagne glasses.
You can find these on the cheap.

What pours out of a bottle is affected by countless factors. Give vintners some props. There's a reason why exceptional bottles fetch well over $1,000. Each bottle of wine is unique, reflecting where the grapes were grown, the fermentation process, whether the wine was oaked (the flavor of the wood barrels the wine absorbs), tannin content (astringent compounds that make you pucker), seasonal glitches, and the vintner's personality. Some wines are purely one grape, others are blends; some are marketed with the cachet of the region they were grown: Bordeaux, Chablis, Napa Valley. All fart-sniffing aside, below are the major wine genres you'll need in your arsenal.

RED WINES

Cabernet Sauvignon
AROMA: Pungent with hints of black currant and grass that punches you in the nose.

FLAVOR: Full-bodied (strong flavor, high in alcohol) with herbaceous flavors like bell peppers, mint, and eucalyptus. It's not for pantywaist wimps desperate to look classy.

GRAPE: Small black with thick, durable skins; high in tannins.

REGION: Everywhere: Bordeaux, Tuscany, Napa Valley, Sonoma County, Australia, your mom's backyard.

PAIRING: Overwhelms delicate or spicy dishes. Stick to meats, burgers, pasta with red sauce, and the woolly mammoth you killed with your bare hands.

Merlot

AROMA: Light and fruity with hints of berry, plum, and currant. Don't you feel pretty now?

FLAVOR: Soft, fruity, and smooth with less tannins; easy for wine-drinking amateurs to enjoy. Just don't tell the guys from *Sideways*.

GRAPE: Large, soft-skinned, dark blue; in loose bunches with less tannins.

REGION: Mostly France, also Napa Valley, Sonoma County, Chile, Argentina, Australia.

PAIRING: Similar to Cabernet. Pair with grilled meats, seafood, greens, mushrooms, and pasta behind closed doors where wine snobs can't mock you.

Pinot Noir

AROMA: Broad bouquet (scent) with hint of fruit. Smells like half your paycheck.

FLAVOR: Delicate, fresh, and voluptuous, aka romantic. The pretentious wino's preferred poison.

GRAPE: Dark red, clustered together in bunches like pinecones.

REGION: Challenging to grow. Grown in cooler regions such as Burgundy, Sonoma County, Willamette Valley, your ex's heart.

PAIRING: Salmon, chicken, lamb, salad, duck, heavy cream sauces, and smug fart-sniffing.

Syrah/Shiraz

AROMA: Depends on aging; from violets, berries, chocolate, and black pepper.

FLAVOR: Intense and full-bodied when young, savory and earthy when aged. Like a hottie that gets her hair cropped short and starts wearing mom jeans once cruel Old Man Time busts his nut on her.

GRAPE: Dark-skinned, grown in clusters; massive tannin content.

REGION: Warmer regions in Australia and France, also United States, Argentina, Chile, South Africa.

PAIRING: Pairs best with peppered meats such as beef, game, stews, sausages, and BBQ. You can always use the bottle to club the animal you plan to eat.

WHITE WINES

Champagne

AROMA: Delicate floral scents, like you're at a wedding, possibly your own.

FLAVOR: Bubbly, crisp, and sweet from sugar added to create carbonation. Drunk by wealthy industrialists and hip-hop moguls in Saint-Tropez.

GRAPE: Made with blend of Chardonnay, Pinot Noir, and Pinot Meunier grapes.

REGION: Technically only the Champagne region of France, but "sparkling wines" abound from around the world.

PAIRING: Oysters, fish, shellfish, appetizers/starters. Also mixes well with cocaine on yachts.

Chardonnay

AROMA: Subtle scent that doesn't overwhelm your nostrils, but reeks of the suburbs.

FLAVOR: Wider body with citrus flavors. Commonly enjoyed by housewives zonked on Xanax.

GRAPE: Malleable green skin that takes on flavors from the oak barrels and soil.

REGION: Most planted grape worldwide. Thrives in France and California regions. Chances are one of your snooty neighbors has a mini-vineyard.

PAIRING: Wide array: poultry, pork, seafood, cream sauces, cheese, garlic, and extramarital affairs.

Riesling

AROMA: Flowery, perfumed scent with hints of fruit like apples, honey, and green grass; like a ballerina gracefully tickling your nostrils and balls.

FLAVOR: Dry, semisweet, tart, fresh, crisp taste due to acidity; lighter than Chardonnay. Drunk before hardcore German porn shoots, especially scheisse films.

GRAPE: Delicate white and takes on characteristics of region where they are grown.

REGION: Colder regions, mostly Germany; also Austria, France, Italy, Australia.

PAIRING: Versatile: fish, pork, chicken, grilled seafood, spicy food, Asian cuisine, and German girls/guys.

Sauvignon Blanc

AROMA: Evokes powerful scents like grapefruit, bell pepper, and fresh-cut grass. Smells like sexy elitism to me, like a porno filmed in the Harvard library.

FLAVOR: Crisp, dry, and refreshing, ranging from tropical sweet to grassy. Enjoyed by those who enjoy ordering it just because it sounds so goddamn classy. Ooh la la!

GRAPE: Green skin that buds late, but ripens early. Doesn't age well, like summer sun sluts.

REGION: Cool climates like Pinots: France, Australia, New Zealand, South Africa, California.

PAIRING: Seafood, poultry, salads, cheese, the only wine that complements sushi. Also pairs well with trust-fund tramps . . . so long as they pay for the bottle.

BEER ME, BITCH!

Back in the days of dragons and jousts and renaissance fairs, people drank beer instead of water because it wouldn't cause dysentery. Suds have been enjoyed with food since ancient Mesopotamia over 5,000 years ago. Beer is produced in many different styles and flavors that range from light and fruity to rich and complex. Wine pairing has stick-up-your-bum rules. Beer pairing is more subjective and laid-back, much like its consumers. Still, you want the beer to complement the food.

Think about what flavor characteristics in the beer stand out or dominate. A thick cut of steak, for example, pairs swimmingly with a rich, dry stout, because a bold flavor like beef needs to be complemented by a big, bold-flavored beer. Sushi pairs well with lighter beers. Amber beers offer relief and flavor balance to spicy foods. Ethnic beers complement ethnic foods.

Types of Beer

There are about as many beers as types of people to bang. But in the beer world, there are two main styles of beer with a million and one permutations. Those are ales and lagers. Think of ale as red wine and lager as white wine with the same general pairing rules. Ale is full-bodied and voluptuous like Kim Kardashian's ass. Lager is more a skinny skank like Keira Knightley (minus pirate wear). There's an occasion for each, you just need to figure out which is right for the occasion. I'm an equal opportunity drinker (and banger).

Ales

Ales are defined by the strain of yeast (not extracted from yeast infections, incidentally) and high temperature used to ferment them. They are more full bodied and fruitier than lagers because of the malt and preserves that went into them. True beer artistry is found within the ale family. Only ingredients and imagination limit the brewer. The same can be said for the pairer. Since you bought this book, you're groovy gravy.

Types of Ale
- Amber ale
- American wheat ale
- Blonde ale
- Brown ale
- Chocolate stout
- Cream ale

- Dry stout
- English brown ale
- Golden ale
- Oatmeal stout
- Old ale
- Hefeweizen
- Imperial stout
- India pale ale
- Irish stout
- Lambics
- Light ale
- Mild ale
- Milk stout
- Pale ale
- Porter
- Red ale
- Scotch ale

Suggested Ale Pairings
- BBQ
- Beef
- Game
- Hamburgers
- Hearty foods
- Lamb
- Pizza
- Sandwiches
- Sausages
- Shepherd's pie
- Strong cheese
- Stews

Lagers

Lagers are the most common form of beer. They dominate the marketplace. Think Budweiser, Miller, and Heineken. Do yourself a favor and don't think Pabst Blue Ribbon or Milwaukee's Best unless you're trying to bang a Hipster Ho-bag. Lagers are inexpensive and plentiful (just like Hipster Hobags). They are lighter beers that can be stored for long periods of time because they are fermented at cooler temperatures. The main styles of lager are pilsner, Vienna, and marzen.

Lager Pairings

- Bratwurst
- Chicken dishes
- Delicate foods
- Ethnic foods
- Fried foods
- Grilled vegetables
- Light cheeses
- Pasta
- Pretzels and mustard
- Soup
- Spicy food
- Sushi
- Vegan food

Libation Lubrication Cheat Sheet

- **Appetizers:** Champagne, Chardonnay
- **Asian food:** Riesling, Sauvignon Blanc, lager, sake
- **BBQ:** Cabernet Sauvignon, Merlot, Syrah, ale
- **Breakfast:** Champagne, mimosa, Bellini, Bloody Mary

- **Cheese:** Chardonnay, Sauvignon Blanc, ale (strong flavor), lager (light)
- **Cream sauces:** Pinot Noir, Chardonnay
- **Desserts:** Champagne, Riesling, port
- **Fish:** Merlot, Pinot Noir, Chardonnay, Riesling, Sauvignon Blanc
- **Fried foods:** Syrah, Champagne, Sauvignon Blanc, Riesling, lager
- **Meat:** Cabernet Sauvignon, Merlot, Pinot Noir, Syrah, ale
- **Pasta:** Cabernet Sauvignon, Merlot, lager
- **Pizza:** Pinot Noir, Syrah, Chardonnay, ale, lager
- **Poultry:** Pinot Noir, Chardonnay, lager
- **Pork:** Cabernet Sauvignon, Merlot, Pinot Noir, Syrah, Chardonnay, Riesling
- **Salads:** Pinot Noir, Sauvignon Blanc
- **Sandwiches:** Pinot Noir, Riesling, ale
- **Sausages:** Syrah, ale, lager
- **Shellfish:** Champagne, Chardonnay, Riesling, lager
- **Spicy food:** Riesling, lager
- **Soup:** Pinot Noir, Chardonnay, Sauvignon Blanc, lager
- **Vegetables:** Merlot, Syrah, Chardonnay, lager

DRINK TO BANG RECIPES

Bangria

The sound of castanets and Flamenco guitar riffs accompany the beautiful figure in a black dress sauntering toward me. Then she's gone. Carmen? I first laid eyes on her in a bar in Valencia, Spain, sipping sangria. Carmen led me onto the dance floor, wrapped her legs around my hips and I melted. She sent me for another round of sangria. When I returned she had vanished. To this day I don't know if she was real or a hallucination brought on by a sangria overdose. So I drink sangria now, hoping she will return. At the very least, I can turn any woman I serve it to into Carmen . . . for the night.

Total time: approximately 2 hours (mostly chilling)
Projected cost: $12
Eating buddy: Beggin' for Bacon-Wrapped Scallops (pages 120–121)
Ingredients:

5 oranges
1 pint strawberries
3 lemons
1 bottle cheap red wine
3 shots vodka
16 ounces your favorite juice (I use strawberry lemonade)

Cut 1 orange into half-moon slices. Take another orange and chop it up into little nibbles. Wash and stem the strawberries and chop up into more nibbles. Throw all the fruit in a punch bowl and squeeze the juice from the remaining oranges and the lemons, throwing away the rinds.

Stir in the red wine, vodka, and juice and put it in the fridge so the fruit chunks soak up the flavor, approximately 2 hours. Fill each glass with ice and ladle in the sangria with the fruit chunks. Drink up. Tell Carmen I say *¡Hola!*

Lick Your Lips Mint Julep

I do declare! Watching Kentucky Derby thoroughbreds sure gets me hot under the collar. The horse racing is nice too. The race is just an excuse for bourgeois people to socialize and fornicate. Naturally, sundresses peeling off in the summer makes you want to cool off with a classic Southern beverage like the mint julep. Play your cards right, mix the drink well, and you could be in for a few furloughs. Hot to fucking trot!

Total time: approximately 30 minutes
Projected cost: $6
Eating buddy: Who Da Mac & Cheese? (pages 141–142)
Ingredients (per drink):
    1 cup water
    2/3 cup white sugar
    1/3 cup brown sugar
    2 sprigs mint leaves
    Crushed ice
    2 shots bourbon

Create a mint simple syrup by boiling the water and mixing in the white and brown sugar until they dissolve. Turn off the heat, throw in a handful of mint leaves and steep in the fridge for 30 minutes.

Frost your serving glass or tin cup. Fill the glass to the brim with crushed ice and stuff in a sprig of mint leaves. Pour in the same amount of bourbon and simple syrup and mix vigorously. Now serve this up to that southern belle or gentleman like your name is Smarty Jones.

Mo' Mojo Mojito

¡Viva la revolución! I'm not talking about Fidel Castro's cigar-chomping communist regime. This is the cocktail revolution led by the magical mojito. This cocktail is liquid sex appeal. The tart of the lime gets your feet moving; the sweet sugar fuels your

libido; the frosty mint refreshes your overheating ass; the rum makes you holler at the moon. Mojitos never fail to arm me with mo' mojo. Much love to the people in Havana who created the perfect excuse to drink until you'd bang a hippo carcass.

Total time: approximately 35 minutes
Projected cost: $5
Eating buddy: Quesa-diddle-ya (page 75)
Ingredients (per drink):
    1 cup water
    ⅔ cup white sugar
    ⅓ cup brown sugar
    1 bunch mint leaves
    1 large handful ice
    ½ lime, quartered
    2 shots light rum
    1 fat splash club soda

Create a mint simple syrup by boiling the water, mixing in the white and brown sugars, and stir until the sugars dissolve. Turn off the heat, throw in a handful of mint leaves, and steep in the fridge for 30 minutes.

Crush the ice in a blender or with an ice pick or fancy refrigerator ice dispenser. Throw half of the lime and 12 mint leaves into a glass. Muddle the shit out of them. I use an ice scream scoop because I'm hardcore.

Throw a handful of the crushed ice, 2 shots of the simple syrup, and muddle like a madman. Pour in the rum, fill the rest of the glass with club soda and garnish it off with more mint leaves. Play some Buena Vista Social Club in the background and salsa until your *pantalónes* slide right off.

Naughty Eggnog

Toxic eggnog is a life raft for awkward holiday moments. This recipe may be just what you need to bring to the holiday office party. If all goes to plan everyone will be too tanked to think of you as anything but a champ. Encourage them to drink up and be merry. Not merry yet? Have another glass of this naughty nog. Serve them enough of this creamy cocktail and they'd forgive you for sexually harassing the water cooler. Homemade eggnog is like holiday Kevlar and you are the drunken baby Jesus.

Total time: approximately 1¼ hours (3 minutes to prep,
   the rest to chill)
Projected cost: $12
Eating buddy: Pinch-Your-Ass-Berry Brownies (pages 73–75)
Ingredients (6 sexy servings):
   6 eggs
   1 cup brown sugar
   1 teaspoon vanilla extract
   Ground nutmeg, to taste
   2 cups heavy cream
   2½ cups whole milk
   ½ cup dark rum
   ½ cup brandy

Add each ingredient separately, in this order, beating them thoroughly: eggs, brown sugar, vanilla extract. After beating it all together, toss in nutmeg.

Add in this order, and mix thoroughly: heavy cream, milk, rum, brandy. Beat together and chill in the fridge for at least 1 hour before serving. After chilling, mix it again and then ladle up glasses and sprinkle with more nutmeg. Ho ho ho!

Not-So-Teeny-Weeny Bellini

It's time you class up your game. Replace the Winnie-the-Pooh nightlight with candles and stop serving your dates Boone's Farm. It's time for this bubbly taste of class known to the civilized world as the Bellini. It's like a Mimosa remix that keeps them coming back for seconds, thirds, and tenths. Serve this with dessert or the morning after a night of carnal consummation. You could also pour it all over your naked body and invite your sweetie to lick you clean. You're a peach!

Total time: approximately 5 minutes

Projected cost: $7

Eating buddy: Huevos Grande Rancheros (page 70) or Sexy Crazy Mofo Tofu Scramble (pages 123–124)

Ingredients:

> 2 ripe peaches
> 1 bottle Champagne
> 1 strawberry

Coarsely chop the peaches. Throw them in a blender with some Champagne and puree.

Cut thin slices of the strawberry and rest them on the edges of 2 Champagne glasses. Pour in half the peach puree and fill the rest with Champagne. Pour gently and allow bubbles to subside before filling to the top. See that person staring back at you in the mirror? I'm so very proud of them.

Panty-Dropping Shandy

The Shandy is a classic colonial British drink that runs the gamut from the mundane beer mixed with 7UP to the insane beer mixed with lighter fluid and shark's blood. This one's a compromise that a one-armed chimp could mix. The garnishes make all the difference. The mint, lime, and lemons are like the tuxedo that covers up a pair of tighty whiteys. Shandys are refreshingly intoxicating and are perfect to cool your hot steamy imperialist ass off while you occupy the territory in your date's pantaloons.

Total time: approximately 5 minutes
Projected cost: $7
Eating buddy: Quesa-diddle-ya (pages 75–76)
Ingredients:
   3 cans of beer
   ½ can frozen lemonade concentrate
   1 lime, cut into small pieces
   1 lemon, cut into small pieces
   1 handful fresh mint leaves

Mix together all the ingredients. Serve the Shandy in clear glasses so your glorious drink can be admired.

Raging Hard (On) Lemonade

Ever have a lemonade stand with a janky misspelled cardboard sign offering LEMMONAID 4 SAIL? Sure your mother did all the work and you only earned thirty-five cents, but you showed entrepreneurial spunk! What a difference a little vodka could have made. Every housewife, teenager, and wino in a five-mile radius would have lined up. If the cops came, you'd just smile all cute and innocent and claim you thought vodka was just "Mommy's special water" and hand the officers a glass. An adult running a suburban lemonade stand is ridiculous. But serve spiked lemonade to a date and unleash their wild child.

> **Total time: approximately 40 minutes**
> **Projected cost: $4 (excluding liquor)**
> **Eating buddy: Friction Chicken Salad (pages 81–82)**
> **Ingredients:**
>> 1 cup water
>> 1½ cups white sugar
>> ½ cup brown sugar
>> 2 sprigs mint, broken up
>> 6 strawberries
>> 2 cups lemon juice (from about 5 lemons)
>> 1 cup vodka
>> Crushed ice

Create a mint simple syrup by boiling the water, mixing in the white and brown sugars, and stir until the sugars dissolve. Turn off the heat, throw in a handful of mint leaves and steep in the fridge for 30 minutes.

Cut the stems off the strawberries and coarsely chop. Cut one strawberry in long strips and line around the glasses. Puree half the coarsely chopped strawberries in a blender. Set the other half aside.

Pour the lemon juice into a big mixing bowl with the simple syrup, the pureed and coarsely chopped strawberries, the vodka, remaining mint, and ice. Mix it all up and serve.

Slutty Temple

Never trust a redhead. This rule applies to the seemingly innocent drink from your childhood. 7UP mixed with grenadine seems innocent enough. Right? That's what I thought when I drank six of them at this crazy ginger girl's apartment. The drink tasted so sweet I didn't realize there was enough vodka in them to kill a rhino. Before I could protest, she had me dressed up in a sailor suit singing a duet:

> "On the drunk ship lolli-whore,
> We took a trip to the liquor store!"

Total time: approximately 2 minutes
Projected cost: $4
Eating buddy: Pesto Bango! Chicken Sinwich (pages 67–68)
Ingredients (per drink):
    1 handful ice
    1 part vodka
    2 parts 7UP
    1 splash grenadine
    1 lime wedge

First ice the glass and then pour in the vodka and 7UP. Add a splash of grenadine so the drink gets red, squeeze a lime wedge and drop into the glass. Stir it all up and serve, you innocent, you.

Smoking Hot Peppermint Fatty

It's colder outside than Ann Coulter's cooch. Your date is keen to stay warm and absorb your body heat. This alcoholic hot cocoa recipe should help you mark a few extra notches on the bedpost until spring fever turns you into rabbits in heat. You get the comfort of a hot chocolate warming the bones while the cocoa aphrodisiac sets the loins ablaze. The warm minty beverage will lower inhibitions and freshen your breath. The two of you should be rolling around in the snow buck-naked in no time.

Total time: approximately 2 minutes
Projected cost: $8
Eating buddy: Pinch-Your-Ass-Berry-Brownies (pages 73–74)
Ingredients:
    1 pint milk or soymilk
    4 ounces bittersweet chocolate
    2 tablespoons sweetened cocoa powder
    3 shots peppermint schnapps
    Whipped cream, to your liking
    2 candy canes

Warm 2 ounces of the milk on very low heat. Chop the chocolate into shards and melt in the milk until it's a divine goop, approximately 4 minutes. Pour in the rest of the milk and add the cocoa and heat up. Make sure to not boil, approximately 2 minutes.

Pour 1½ shots of the peppermint schnapps into each mug and top them off with the homemade cocoa. Serve with whipped cream. Add the candy cane if you're infected by the holiday spirit.

7

Sexual Profiling

Now that you've learned the ropes, it's time to get out in the field. There are all kinds of people out there to bang. Skinny ones, curvy ones, sexy ones, and homely ones we would never admit to banging. (It was the whiskey, damnit!) It takes all kinds. Each type has their own palate.

Cook to Bang works for anyone, but it requires customizing the formula as needed. A hipster you find at an indie rock show will have vastly different tastes than a redneck you meet at church. Your challenge is to figure out whom you are cooking for and what they like.

Don't serve a vegan feminist activist veal milanese and call her "baby." You might end up with a candlelit Take Back the Night vigil outside your place rather than an evening shattering misplaced taboos. A great chef adapts their recipes to please the pickiest of patrons. That's why you should identify whom or what you are dealing with so you know what food to make and how to make your move.

Everyone thinks they're a unique snowflake, but the reality is that there are *types*. There are always exceptions to the rule and I'm sure you are that special individual your mother said you were. Fair enough. But for our purposes, we're going to deal with all those photocopies that can't bother to distinguishing themselves the way you have. Nice belt, by the way. I got the same one at Urban Outfitters.

The upside to dating someone who can be compartmentalized is the formula for seducing them. They share certain quirks, attitudes, and tastes. All you need is the combination to unlock their chastity belts. Chastity belts worn by Club Sluts and Hipster Ho-bags are cheaply made knockoffs from Malaysian sweatshops. They can be removed with a compliment and a drink. A Holy Hottie's chastity belt requires the persistence of a safe-cracking jewel thief. But they can all be opened with the right amount of gumption.

Think of your meal as a distraction, like a parade during a bank heist. Your date will be too engaged in the delicious food and stunning conversation to realize their vault has been pried open. You will have already purloined the jewels and gold doubloons in their pantaloons before they realize your true intentions. At that point the seal has been broken, so a repeat visit to the vault is assured. Now it's time to familiarize yourself with the targets and formulate your scheme.

HOLY HOTTIES

I've had impure thoughts in many a house of God. Churches, temples, and mosques—I've desecrated them all . . . in my mind. I have yet to fornicate in a confession booth—maybe this Sunday—but I love banging the bejesus out of good Christian girls. Make like a snake offering forbidden fruit, throw a condom in the collection plate, and make them cry, "Hallelujah!"

Pros

- **Gullible:** They live by faith in something they can't see or prove.
- **Cheap date:** Jesus was a humble man. You're the dating answer to WWJD?
- **All sins are forgiven:** Just bend over and pray.

Cons

- **Challenge to seduce:** Sex on the first date can be challenging without an engagement ring or the Virgin Mary appearing in your French toast.
- **They cry after sex:** Makes it awkward when you ask them to leave.
- **Not always worth effort:** It's an onward Christian soldier's duty not to bang.

How to Spot a Holy Hottie

Chicks
Eyes on the prize, aka the Lord
Pearl necklace (not that kind)
Bible in hand
Purity ring
Crucifix necklace
Sundress with cleavage
Conservative clompy shoes

Dudes
Penny loafers
Pressed khaki pants
Blue blazer

Hair with a part
Argyle socks
Tucked-in shirt

Where to Pick Up Holy Hotties
- Bingo night in the church basement
- Starbucks on a Saturday night
- Antiabortion rallies

How to Bang Holy Hotties
- Proclaim that God commanded you to bang them.
- Perform a passion play between the sheets.
- Make them think you will propose (then DON'T!).

What Holy Hotties Eat
Holy Hotties have simple tastes like their Lord and savior. Don't get all Blue Statey serving anything too gourmet, or worse, French-sounding. Think, "What would Jesus do?" Turn water into wine, a whole lot of wine.

Oh God, Don't Stop! Jalapeño Poppers
There's a reason why people cry out for their maker when they are getting pounded with pleasure. Orgasms are as close as us mere mortals will ever get to God. But "Oh Gods" aren't exclusive to sex. We've all cried out something similar when biting into a piece of heaven. Once you jalapeño popper, you can't stop her! Get 'em baking and shit starts shaking. These portable 'peños are perfect for church potlucks, tabernacle tailgating, and sanctified swinger parties. Praise the goddamn Lord!

Total time: approximately 15 minutes

Projected cost: $4

Drinking wingman: Sparkling holy water (aka vodka soda)
   or holy brew

Ingredients:

   2 handfuls shredded Jack cheese

   3 ounces cream cheese

   1 tablespoon honey

   5 jalapeños, split lengthwise and seeds and veins removed

   1 egg

   2 teaspoons milk

   ½ teaspoon paprika

   ⅓ cup flour

   ⅓ cup breadcrumbs

Preheat the oven to 350°F. Mix the Jack and cream cheese with the honey. Fill the hollow jalapeños with the cheese mixture.

Mix together the egg, milk, and paprika. Set out the flour, egg mixture, and breadcrumbs in separate bowls. Dip each cheesy jalapeño first in flour, then egg mixture, and finally the breadcrumbs. Arrange in a foil-covered baking pan.

Shove the baking pan full of prepped jalapeños into the oven. Bake until the breading browns and the cheese begins to ooze out the sides, approximately 30 minutes. Serve them up on a platter with your favorite condom-ments.

Sinful Salvation Salad

Praise the Lor . . . no wait . . . praise the whores! May the sinners of the world indulge without fear of reprisal from cock-blocking conservatives. Who are they to say what body parts you can or can't slather in salad dressing? Do my nipples smothered in Japanese miso dressing condemn me to eternal damnation? Fear not the reprisals from an angry God bent on you burning in hellfire with sharp pitchforks piercing your soft bum. Indulge without risking tainting your soul or your healthy diet regimen. Feel no shame for you are loved. Amen.

Total time: approximately 10 minutes
Projected cost: $7
Drinking wingman: blood of God (red wine from chalice)
Ingredients:
    ½ head butter lettuce
    1 hardboiled egg
    1 baked chicken breast
    1 tomato, cut into wedges
    ½ avocado, thinly sliced
    1 handful dried cranberries
    Japanese miso salad dressing

Chop the lettuce into bite-size pieces. Thinly slice the hardboiled egg. Cut the chicken into long strips.

Lay out each salad in this order: lettuce, tomato, avocado, chicken, egg, cranberries, and lastly salad dressing at your discretion.

YUMMY YUPPIES

"You down with G-O-P? Yeah, you know me!" screamed the Yummy Yuppie in the power pantsuit I picked up crashing a Republican ball in Washington, D.C. She's part of the new generation of go-get-'em-and-thumb-fuck-their-eyeballs-if-they-get-in-your-way school. The love child of Gordon Gekko and Ivanka Trump. Their sexual compulsions match their ambition making them perfect targets for Cook to Bang.

Pros

- **No time for relationship:** They just want to bang before 10 A.M. conference call.
- **Sugar mamas/daddies:** They might buy you shit if you cook and bang well.
- **Indifference to infidelity:** They won't notice or care if you bang other people.

Cons

- **Power tripping:** They need to be in control at all times, which is emasculating.
- **Sociopathic delusions of grandeur:** Think Patrick Bateman in *American Psycho*.
  - **BlackBerry = dildo:** They get way more pleasure from their PDA than they do from you.

How to Spot a Yummy Yuppie

Chicks
Hair conservatively pinned back
Power suit
CrackBerry in hand
Suntan from weekend at beach house
Sexy designer briefcase
Jimmy Choo shoes

Dudes
Rolex, referred to as "my Rolex"
AmEx black card in pocket
Prada belt with logo on buckle
Distressed Diesel jeans
Silk shirt from A/X
A. Testoni loafers

Where to Pick Up Yummy Yuppies

- Pottery Barn or Crate & Barrel
- Wine tastings
- Young Republicans events

How to Bang Yummy Yuppies

- Brag about your latest 401(k) contribution.
- Trash-talk Obama and his effect on the market.
- Offer them a ride in your BMW . . . "when it's out of the shop."

What Yummy Yuppies Eat

Yummy Yuppies are the most pretentious, picky eaters. They are foodies, or at least think they are, with cash to afford the best. You better impress them with gourmet "holy-fucking-shit!" quality food in order to Cook to Bang these corporate killers.

Baked Briez Nuts

Your idea of wine and cheese may be a box of Franzia and Cheez Whiz on a Ritz. That won't work for these power trippers. Break out the Brie and declare, "I am indeed sophisticated and quite possibly speak French . . . when I'm not freelancing as an art appraiser for the royal family." Throw in walnuts caramelized in brown sugar on a bed of pears and your dish becomes a member of the cultural elite. If baked Brie served with bread and a bottle of Cabernet won't get the job done with the corporate set, I suggest you credit default swap your genitals for AIG stock.

Total time: approximately 35 minutes
Projected cost: $9
Drinking wingman: Sauvignon Blanc or Cabernet
Ingredients:
> **1 tablespoon unsalted butter**
> **5 thin slices pear**
> **1 wedge Brie**
> **2 tablespoons brown sugar**
> **1 handful crushed walnuts**

Preheat oven to 300°F. Grease a baking pan with a little of the butter and create a bed of pear slices for the Brie to sit on. Spread the rest of the butter over the Brie. Spread the brown sugar evenly over the Brie and crown it with walnuts like royalty.

Bake in the oven until the brown sugar caramelizes and the cheese becomes supple as a vestal virgin, approximately 30 minutes. Serve with slices of French bread or crackers. Let your Yummy Yuppie's greed consume them and soon you will feel as used as one of their summer interns.

Beggin' for Bacon-Wrapped Scallops

It all started while housesitting a family friend's home in Key West. I took a booze cruise along the Florida Bay and met a yuppie girl visiting her parents. We laughed and drank and were ravenous when we stepped off the SS *Drunk Douche*. I bought freshly shucked jumbo scallops from a fisherman on the docks and lured her to my pseudo-abode with promises of the "best meal ever." But the fridge had only condiments and frozen bacon. Desperation led to innovation—and then fornication. Remember to wrap it up tight, son!

Total time: approximately 30 minutes
Projected cost: $15
Drinking wingman: beer, Riesling, Chardonnay,
    Champagne, or Bangria (pages 100–101)
Ingredients:
    2 cloves garlic, finely chopped
    1 tablespoon minced sun-dried tomatoes
    1/2 lemon
    1 tablespoon mayonnaise
    1/2 teaspoon salt
    1/2 teaspoon crushed red pepper flakes
    6 jumbo scallops
    6 strips bacon (pig, turkey, or veggie)

Preheat the oven to 350°F. Mix up the garlic, sun-dried to-matoes, juice from the lemon, mayonnaise, salt, and red pepper flakes in a bowl. Toss the scallops to evenly coat.

Wrap each scallop with a strip of bacon and secure it by piercing the middle with a toothpick. Set the scallops in a small baking pan. Reserve marinade.

Bake the scallops until the coating is brown, approximately 10 minutes. Flip them over, pour the marinade over them and bake until that side is brown, approximately 5 minutes. Serve three to a plate and pour the juice from the pan evenly over the scallops.

HIPPIE HARLOTS

I can still smell the patchouli from my last trip down the un-shaven rabbit hole. Don't get me wrong: Hippie Harlots have given me some of my favorite fantasy fuck files. But at what cost? I became a long hair for a time, with wide-eyed delusions of a peaceful world fueled by psychedelics and jam band music. To my family's glee, I let go of that self-indulging Day-Glo dream. But that doesn't stop me from occasionally trolling Haight-Assbury for bohemian booty.

Pros
- **Slutty by nature:** Hippies go with the flow like they're at a Woodstock gangbang.
- **Killer stash:** Hippies always have amusing ways to kill brain cells.
- **Easy to blow off:** These love children are incapable of mature relationships.

Cons

- **Expiration date:** Cute when young, but like a good jam, these looks "fade away."
- **Not well kempt:** Bring a machete before exploring their nether regions.
- **New roommate:** They might end up crashing with you and never leave.

How to Spot a Hippie Harlot

Chicks
Sacred headband
No makeup
Hairy armpits/legs
Beaded necklace blessed by shaman
No bra
Smells like lavender and BO
Barefoot

Dudes
Birkenstocks referred to as "Birks"
Nappy white-boy dreads
Scraggly beard
Glass bong that's like a girlfriend
Embroidered shirt from spiritual journey to India
Stretched earlobes

Where to Pick Up Hippie Harlots

- San Francisco
- Ultimate Frisbee games
- Burning Man

How to Bang Hippie Harlots

- Feed them anything organic and vegan.
- Play them a rare Phish bootleg from their Burlington days.
- Suggest a tantric yoga exercise only possible without clothes.

What Hippie Harlots Eat

It's a challenge to please Hippie Harlots' moral outrage with traditional taste-rules-all culinary techniques. Many are vegetarians, vegans, or the obnoxious raw foodists. Yet plenty of hippie-crites still eat seafood or eggs. When in doubt, cook vegan. Most aphrodisiacs fit the bill. Now tap that bohemian ass!

Sex Crazy Mofo Tofu Scramble

The upside to banging a Hippie Harlot is their free loving attitude (aka bang you on the first date). The brutal downside is misguided eating restrictions based on nonsense they wholeheartedly believe . . . until they inevitably become their parents. So you spent an evening hiding the salami in every orifice Mother Earth manifested. Come morning, they recoil at your screwed-your-brains-out-scrambled-eggs, and lecture you about the poor piggies who died so your bacon could sizzle. The solution: scrambled tofu, a goddamn delicious vegan compromise. Please the shiny happy people who will then please the frisky horny people.

Total time: approximately 10 minutes
Projected cost: $7
Drinking wingman: Not-So-Teeny-Weeny Bellini (page 105)
Ingredients:
    2 cloves garlic, minced
    ½ onion, coarsely chopped
    1 tablespoon olive oil

1 handful cilantro leaves
1 tomato, coarsely chopped
2 handfuls spinach
½ pound firm tofu
½ avocado, thinly sliced

Sauté the garlic and onions in the oil on medium-high heat until they become translucent, approximately 2 minutes. Throw in the cilantro, tomato, and spinach and sauté until they go limp, approximately 3 minutes.

Cut the tofu into cubes, toss them into the pan, and scramble like a champion until the flavor sets in and the tofu breaks apart, approximately 3 minutes. Serve up on a plate, crowning it with the avocado slices.

Dank Organic Veggie Burritos

Holy shit, bra! Did you catch Phish at Bonaroo? I mean, like, whoa! Maybe I'll be more articulate once the acid wears off. Anyway, I picked up TWO hard-body Hippie Harlots in the lot while selling Dank Organic Veggie Burritos out of my mom's Prius. I played them some old bootlegs from, like, WAY back in the day. They were mad impressed, especially when they started rubbing the Phish tat I've got on my heart. Good thing they didn't realize it was henna until after we knocked Birkenstocks.

Total time: approximately 15 minutes
Projected cost: $8
Drinking wingman: Panty-Dropping Shandy
    (spiked with LSD, if possible; page 106)
Ingredients:
    2 cloves garlic, finely chopped

1 tablespoon olive oil

1 onion, cut into strips

1 red bell pepper, cut into strips

1 green bell pepper, cut into strips

2 dashes fajita seasoning

Burrito-size tortillas

Cooked rice

1 (16-ounce) can black beans, heated

2 handfuls lettuce, cut into strips

1 tomato, coarsely chopped

½ avocado, thinly sliced

Mango salsa

Sauté the garlic in the oil over medium heat for 30 seconds. Throw in the onion and bell peppers. Sprinkle some fajita seasoning and sauté until the vegetables soften, approximately 4 minutes.

Assemble the burritos: Warm the tortillas in the oven and fill each with small scoops of rice, beans, sautéed veggies, lettuce, tomatoes, avocado and mango salsa, if you're feeling adventurous.

Roll up each burrito. Flip one-third of the flap over to cover the ingredients, fold over the left and right side, roll the final flap over and press it so it stays shut. Cut the burritos in half or eat whole like a bohemian barbarian.

HIPSTERS HO-BAGS

Every time I indulge in this flesh, I do so ironically. But then I do the walk of shame thinking, "Fucking hipsters." This scourge of kids in pants so tight they cut off the circulation to their brains is the lowest point on the devolutionary scale. Nothing unites this tribe double-dipped in pretension save for indifference—that and cocaine. Neither their trust-funded emulation of the working

class nor their obsession with the awesome 80s offer true salva-
tion. All hipsters have is the church of irony and, fortunately,
their love of boozing and banging.

Pros

- **Drunky McDrunkle:** You can rely on your hipster date
  to get trashed and frisky.
- **Ironic palette:** Hipsters will eat almost anything if it
  seems weird, different, or retro.
- **Booty call central:** Hipsters are always out late and up
  for late night rendezvous.

Cons

- **Hate everything:** Nothing gets a hipster pumped like
  discussing what sucks.
- **Ugly is beautiful:** Even the hot ones dress dowdy, like
  bag ladies or hobos.
  - **Pretension is their middle name:**
    Their existence is a stream of
    contrivances.

How to Spot a Hipster Ho-bag

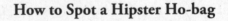

Chicks
Unkempt/unwashed hair
Nonprescription glasses
Always smoking
Vintage T-shirt
Tattoos (hidden) to piss off rich daddy
Skinny jeans rolled into cuffs
Trashed Converse aka Chucks

Dudes

Silly hat that doesn't fit right

Comb-over covering eye

Ridiculous mustache

Ironic American Apparel T-shirt

Can of Pabst Blue Ribbon

Tight jeans strangling gonads

Where to Pick Up Hipster Ho-Bags

- Williamsburg, Silver Lake, the Mission, Wicker Park, and a gentrified neighborhood near you!
- Dive bars
- Warehouse parties

How to Bang Hipster Ho-bags

- Trash-talk any band that has enjoyed commercial success.
- Ask them, "Want to go back to my place, blow lines, and fuck?"
- Buy a six-pack of Pabst Blue Ribbon.

What Hipster Ho-bags Eat

Hipster Ho-bags follow offbeat diet trends, whether that means macrobiotic carnivore or a strict regimen of cake frosting and birth control pills. Don't worry. Your hipster date will be too busy waxing poetic about Godard movies to give much thought to what you serve them. Just let them do their thing and you will surely do your thing.

Señorita Lupita's Cactus Fajitas

Can't a fajita just be filled with peppers, onions, and meat? Not so when dealing with the irony-obsessed hipster populace. Or so I learned at the Austin City Limits festival. This kooky local Lupita I met challenged me to cook her something crazy. We crashed into a cactus on her moped on our way home. So I took nopales (cactus pads), removed the spikes, and stir-fried them. The result was this random, tasty, totally ironic late-night snack that blew Señorita Lupita's mind. She blew something of mine in return. Now one of my exes lives in Texas.

Total time: approximately 15 minutes
Projected cost: $7
Drinking wingman: cerveza or Bangria (pages 100–101)
Ingredients:
    2 teaspoons fajita seasoning
    1 pound chicken, cut into bite-size strips
    2 tablespoons olive oil
    1 nopale
    1 onion, cut into long strips
    1 tomato, coarsely chopped
    6 corn tortillas
    1 handful shredded Jack cheese
    ½ avocado, sliced
    Salsa

Rub 1 teaspoon of fajita seasoning into the chicken and allow the flavor to absorb, approximately 5 minutes. Stir-fry the chicken with 1 tablespoon of the oil and cook through. Set chicken aside.

Slice off the nopale's spikes, skin, and edges, then cut it into long strips. Heat the remaining oil in a pan and stir-fry the onion until softened, approximately 2 minutes. Add the cactus, tomatoes, and remaining fajita seasoning and cook until the tomatoes are stewed, approximately 4 minutes.

Lay out the tortillas, cheese, avocado, and salsa, creating a fajita filling station Even a vegan can assemble something unobjectionable. There will be plenty of objectionable activities later.

Sexier Than Dead Elvis Sinwich

Elvis has left the building . . . in a body bag. Too many fried peanut butter and banana sandwiches, I suppose. I can't explain it, but hipsters love them some Elvis. Must be the irony associated with his gold lamé suit, mutual love of pills, and consumption of odd foods sure to leave you bloated and possibly dead on the shitter. *Cook to Bang* does not endorse this behavior nor the hipster lifestyle. But this sandwich is a delicious lark to share with your hipster lover after an ironic banging session. Just be sure to crank some Elvis tunes, you hunk a hunk of burning love. (That burning is chlamydia, by the way.)

Total time: approximately 8 minutes
Projected cost: $3
Drinking wingman: milkshake with a fistful of barbiturates
Ingredients:
    1 tablespoon unsalted butter
    4 slices bread
    4 tablespoons peanut butter
    1 banana
    2 tablespoons honey

Spread the butter on one side of each slice of bread. Spread the peanut butter on the other side of each slice of bread. Cut the banana lengthwise into 4 thin slices and lay them across the peanut-butter side of each sandwich. Smother the bananas in honey.

Push each sandwich half together. Heat a pan up on medium heat. Place each sandwich in the pan and cook each side until it is golden brown, flipping once. Remove from the pan and cut in half and serve it up, preferably with some Elvis line: "Thank you. Thank you very much!"

CLUB SLUTS AND DANCE FLOOR D-BAGS

You know the type. Red velvet ropes, bottle service, and the desperate cry, "I'm on the DJ's list!" Club kids look so bangable on the dance floor shaking their asses. But don't let their awesome drugs fool you into thinking a Club Slut or Dance Floor D-bag is relationship material. Once you sober up from your eighth Red Bull vodka you will realize they live in a shallow bubble of after-parties and last night's regrets. That doesn't mean you shouldn't bang them recklessly—just triple-wrap your shit.

Pros
- **Smoking hot:** They hone their hard bodies with hard dancing and harder drugs.
- **Don't eat food:** They'll eat any pill you hand them, but are never hungry.
- **Dance floor whores:** If they like your look or smell money, it's so ON!

Cons
- **No direct sunlight:** The Club Slut you banged might look weathered in the light of day.

- **Mood swings:** The drugs, booze, and sex-binging make their hormones go crazy.
- **Typhoid Mary/Mark:** Skanky behavior has resulted in a bigger variety of venereal diseases than designer drugs.

How to Spot a Club Slut or Dance Floor D-bag

Chicks
Glow sticks, rave on!
Ecstasy hit on tongue
Herpes cold sore
Vomit caked in hair extensions
Short skirt, no panties
Tramp stamp tattoo (hidden)
Fuck-me-now pumps

Dudes
Tight-fitting silk shirt
Gelled-up frosted tips
Wristband from last night's club
Attention seeking blah blah bling
Teeth grinding from third E
Red Bull vodka

Where to Pick Up Club Sluts and Dance Floor D-bags
- Anywhere you find loud repetitive music: clubs, concerts, bars, back of a van
- Your drug dealer's pad
- VD clinic

How to Bang Club Sluts and Dance Floor D-bags

- Invite them to your bottle service table (pretend you're with paying D-bags).
- Wear flashy shit and grind like a frat boy on Viagra.
- Say you know the promoter and can hook them up VIP no problem, baby!

What Club Sluts and Dance Floor D-bags Eat

One advantage of cooking to bang a Club Slut or Dance Floor D-bag is they don't really eat. Distorted body issues and a continuous flow of blow curtail their appetites. The upside is a hot body; the downside is volatile, trashy outbursts. Your best bet is to serve light, simple food that is easy to digest when you've got them sweating out on the dance floor—or on your bedroom floor.

In-slut-ada Caprese

There is no social genre easier to manipulate into a threesome than the clubbing set. It seems bisexuality is a prerequisite for being on the guest list. So before (or after) a night out imbibing all manner of intoxicants, inspire them with a simple edible threeway we can all agree on. The hunkiness of good buffalo mozzarella (or burrata if you can afford bottle service) will bring out the bicuriosity of the tomato and basil. This trifecta's sex appeal won't stop until your own trifecta sobers up. You won't be sleeping alone with this salad thrown into the mix. The challenge is fitting them all into your bed.

Total time: 5 minutes
Projected cost: $8
Drinking wingman: Sauvignon Blanc or Red Bull vodka

Ingredients:

> 2 tomatoes, cut into ½-inch slices
> 2 buffalo mozzarella balls, cut into ½-inch rounds
> Fresh basil leaves
> 1 tablespoon balsamic vinegar
> 1 tablespoon olive oil

Stack small towers of tomato, mozzarella, and basil.

Serve up your In-slut-ada Caprese on a plate and drizzle with the desired amount of oil and vinegar. Serve solo, with fresh bread or with newly cracked glowsticks.

Eggs Whorentine

The majority of Club Sluts qualify as whores or, at very least, possess whorish qualities. Bear in mind, I'm not saying "whore" like it's a bad thing. Far from it. Club Sluts already beg the bouncer to let them into the club, the DJ for their latest remix, and the dealer for free drugs. It's only fitting that they should be begging you for their next fix. No doubt, they have burned through countless calories between dancing all night and banging all morning. Time to reload your love machines with protein in the eggs, carbohydrates in the English muffin, and the famed Popeye power of spinach to keep you going long and strong. It's a supply-and-demand thing. Make like OPEC: don't hand over your commodities until they've sucked up enough.

Total time: approximately 10 minutes
Projected cost: $4
Drinking Wingman: Mimosa, Not-So-Teeny-Weeny Bellini
   (page 105), or both

Ingredients:

> 1 shallot, diced
> 2 tablespoons butter
> 3 dashes salt
> 2 healthy handfuls spinach
> ½ lemon
> 3 eggs
> 1 teaspoon Dijon mustard
> 1 dash cayenne pepper
> 1 English muffin, split
> ½ avocado, thinly sliced
> Fresh basil leaves, cut into strips

Sauté the shallot in ½ tablespoon of the butter with a dash of salt until they caramelize, approximately 11 minutes. Toss in the spinach, squeeze ¼ of the juice from the lemon, and cook until the liquid reduces, approximately 4 minutes.

Create the hollandaise sauce. Melt the remaining butter on low heat. Separate the yolk from 1 egg (crack egg in half and pour contents back and forth between shells until the egg whites drip away and only the yolk remains) and mix it up with the mustard, remaining lemon juice, melted butter, and cayenne pepper. Whisk it up into frothy awesomeness.

Toast the English muffin. Now poach the eggs. My method is to gently crack the eggs into a thin layer of water boiling in a pan, using a spatula to create 2 separate eggs. Poach until the egg whites harden and the yolks remain gooey, approximately 3 minutes.

Once the English muffins are toasted, butter them. Place half the spinach on each muffin, following it up with a poached egg. Smother it all with hollandaise sauce and then crown it with the avocado and basil. Breakfast of fucking champions!

SORORITEASES AND FRAT-HOLES

Rushing, pledges, hazing, hell week: It's *Revenge of the Nerds* come to life. Boozing and banging define American university Greek life. When I was getting higher with my education, I crashed many a frat party chasing free beer and sluts. It's a cliquey, tight-knit society sowing their drunken oats before they go establishment. These are the future insurance agents and hedge-funders honing their networking skills between keg stands and goat-fucking. Be wary, for most Sororiteases are pursuing their MRS. degree.

Pros

- *Girls Gone Wild*: Never ending supply of supple young flesh eager to bang.
- **Girl on girl:** Sororiteases are always down to make out with each other.
- **Low self-esteem:** Easy to bang because they wallow in a pool of insecurity.

Cons

- **Sense of entitlement:** Spoiled and whiny because their parents never said no.
- **Groupthink:** They do everything as a group; this is a plus and a minus . . .
- **Carbon copies:** It's a clusterfuck picking yours out from the sea of Xeroxes.

How to Spot a Sororitease
or Frat-hole

Chicks

Makeup smeared from puking
Eyes roving for future husband
Shell necklace from spring break
in Cancún
Pregnancy test in hand
Keg cup full of roofie colada
Black fuck-me-pants, the Sororitease
uniform

Dudes

Backward baseball cap
Bloody nose from coke problem
Polo shirts with flipped collar
Spare tire from keggers
Khaki cargo shorts
Frat symbol tattooed on ankle

Where to Pick Up Sororiteases and Frat-holes
- Tailgating before the game
- Beer pong tournaments
- Wherever cheap beer is found

How to Bang Sororiteases and Frat-holes
- Challenge them to a beer shotgun race.
- Offer them beads to show their tits/cock.
- Brag about your internship at Goldman Sachs.

What Sororiteases and Frat-holes Eat

The eating habits of Sororiteases and Frat-holes are similar to those of the all-American Holy Hotties. Most Greeks are too busy partying to bother with gourmet food. It distracts them from their main objective: to get fucked up and get fucked. They prefer foods that go well with booze and sports. Think grilled meat and cold pizza. Veggies are for fags!

Chicken Wingman

Some guys are breast men, others are leg men; I'm a wingman. My single friends can attest to my ability to help them create connections that lead to copulation. That's what friends do. This is why frat brothers and sorority sisters stay friends forever. After you've jumped on the homely grenade so your amigo could tap some primo ass, they are in debt to you. I won't lie and say chicken wings are classy. But if you have yourself a sports fan that wants to watch the game between banging marathons, this recipe is for you.

> **Total time: approximately 20 minutes**
> **Projected cost: $7**
> **Drinking wingman: booze out of a red plastic cup**
> **Ingredients:**
>> **2 pounds chicken wings and drumettes**
>> **1 teaspoon black pepper**
>> **1 teaspoon salt**
>> **½ tablespoon chili oil**
>> **2 green onions, chopped**
>> **2 jalapeños, chopped and seeds removed**
>> **3 ounces frozen orange juice concentrate, thawed**

1 tablespoon brown sugar
1 tablespoon honey

Preheat the oven to broil. Season the chicken with black pepper, salt, and chili oil. Set aside.

Mix together the green onions, jalapeños, orange juice concentrate, sugar and honey in a deep pan. Cook the mixture on medium-high heat until it reduces to half its original volume, approximately 3 minutes.

Toss the chicken with the sauce mixture, drain, and set in a baking pan. Broil the chicken until each side browns, flipping them halfway through, 5 to 6 minutes per side. Cook the chicken wings in saucepan over medium heat until the sauce glazes on each wing. Now serve it all up. Game on!

Sloppy (Seconds) Joes

Ever hear the expression "Tri-Delta. Everyone else has"? Chances are, if you were in the Greek system in college, you will bang someone all your friends have banged. No shame in hitting it after your friends, unless it was on the same night without protection and now there's a post-frat-gangbang love child. Keep it under wraps and don't allow this booty call to evolve into a five-year relationship. Friendships are way more important than some discarded strange anyway. But sloppy isn't always bad. Sloppy can be damn good when stuffed into a bread roll and smothered with avocado. Embrace the tangy terrific taste of a Sloppy (Seconds) Joe without shame or fear of retribution.

Total time: approximately 30 minutes
Projected cost: $15

**Drinking Wingman: beer or a Raging Hard (On) Lemonade
(pages 106–107)**
Ingredients:

    ½ teaspoon crushed garlic

    2 tablespoons olive oil

    2 green peppers, coarsely chopped

    1 pound ground beef or turkey

    ½ teaspoon salt

    2 large dried chiles, coarsely chopped

    1 can beer

    ½ cup ketchup

    1 tablespoon Worcestershire sauce

    2 green onions, coarsely chopped

    2 sandwich rolls

    ½ avocado, thinly sliced

Sauté the garlic in the oil in a stockpot over medium heat for a few seconds, before throwing in the bell peppers, meat, and salt. Cook and stir, breaking up the meat, until it is browned, approximately 5 minutes.

Add the chopped chiles and cook until the flavor releases, approximately 2 minutes. Pour in the beer, ketchup, and Worcestershire sauce and cook until the liquids thicken, approximately 20 minutes. Turn the heat off and add the green onions.

Split each roll down the middle, leaving the base intact. Spoon in the Sloppy Joe mixture, crowning it with avocado and serve it up sloppy, Joe.

NASCAR NASTIES

The popular misconception is that all NASCAR fans are po' white trash living in trailers in the South. This is way wrong!

That's just most of them. Rednecks can be found all over the United States including California, Florida, even New York. What they all share is a love for stock car racing, guns and unwed teenage mothers. God bless this salt of the earth who understand the true value of a beer cozy.

Pros

- **Easy to seduce:** No man in their life never cooked *them* no damn meal!
- **Farmer's daughter/stable boy fantasy:** Take a roll in the hay they baled.
- **Can gut a pig:** This will come in handy should civilization collapse during the course of your date.

Cons

- **Short shelf life:** Too much boozing, sun, and inhaling exhaust fumes.
  - **Pro-lifers:** No get-out-of-paying-child-support-for-eighteen-years-free card.
  - **Their daddy is armed:** Here comes the bride.

How to Spot a NASCAR Nasty

Chicks
Black eye from her man
Blank stare from inbreeding
Plaid top stained with fluids
Pre-baby-bump belly button exposed
Daisy Dukes!
Cowboy boots, y'all!

Dudes

Baseball cap from their race team
Oakley sunglasses with strap
Chewing-tobacco-packed lips
Sleeveless promotional T-shirt
Beer gut
Tattoo of baby mama's name

Where to Pick Up a NASCAR Nasty

- Racetrack
- County fair
- NRA rally

How to Bang a NASCAR Nasty

- Compliment their (gun) rack.
- Claim you were a rodeo clown.
- Tell them your stick shift goes up to seven.

What NASCAR Nasties Eat

Fancy food need not apply, y'all. NASCAR Nasties want food "real people" eat. I'm not sure what that means, but a roommate in college said it is the opposite of what I cook. I'm pretty sure it involves shopping for produce at Walmart. Keep it simple and fattening.

Who da Mac & Cheese?

This dish turns a white trash classic on its head. Truth be told, I hate mac & cheese from the box. It harkens back to my time spent in a wilderness reform program getting the shit kicked out of me by former drug addict born-agains (yes, I was a troubled youth). The flavor and texture are as bland as Kansas. But done right, mac & cheese will complement any all-American meal from fried chicken to pork chops. The bountiful bevy of cheeses and the spicy jalapeño will grab your date's attention and create a sexy barn dance in your mouths. America, love it, or leave it hungry for more!

Total time: approximately 75 minutes
Projected cost: $12
Drinking wingman: cheap beer, whiskey, Lick Your Lips Mint
    Julep (pages 101–102), or milk for their kid in tow
Ingredients:
    2 cups macaroni
    2 tablespoons unsalted butter
    1 tablespoon flour
    2 teaspoons salt
    1 cup milk
    2 jalapeños: 1½ chopped, ½ cut into rounds
    ½ onion, finely chopped
    1 cup shredded mozzarella
    1 (1-inch-thick) round goat cheese
    1 cup grated Gouda
    2 tablespoons breadcrumbs
    Hot sauce

Preheat the oven to 350°F. Boil a pot of water and cook the macaroni, approximately 10 minutes. Once macaroni is al dente, drain the pasta in a colander.

Melt the butter in a deep pan on medium-low heat. Add the flour and salt and slowly mix in the milk. Cook until the milk thickens. Add the chopped jalapeños and onion and cook them into the now thickened sauce. Finally throw in all three cheeses and mix together.

Pour the macaroni mixture into a greased baking dish. Place the sliced jalapeños on top and sprinkle with the breadcrumbs. Bake until the breadcrumb crust is browned, 35 to 45 minutes. Serve with hot sauce.

Frisky Krispies

The roar of the NASCAR engines makes fans moist and frisky. A better time to pounce with delicious, easy-to-make treats there could not be! These krispies are turbo-charged with raspberry antioxidant nitro blasts like Dale Jr.'s No. 88 stock car. They will keep you vroom-vroom-vrooming until your NASCAR Nasty's spouse comes home early from their hunting trip. These treats are tasty enough to slow them down so you can escape out their trailer's bathroom window, avoiding the world famous *Deliverance*-style Southern hospitality.

> **Total time: approximately 40 minutes**
> **Projected cost: $6**
> **Drinking wingman: hot cocoa**
> **Ingredients:**
> > **¼ stick unsalted butter (2 tablespoons)**
> > **10 ounces marshmallows**
> > **6 cups Rice Krispies (generic okay)**
> > **1 pint fresh raspberries**

Melt the butter on low heat. Stir in the marshmallows until they become a goop, approximately 5 minutes.

Turn off the heat and mix in the krispies and raspberries. Dump the mixture into a greased baking pan, pat them down with a spatula, and allow them to cool, approximately 30 minutes. Cut up the squares and distribute to your conquests.

8

Setting the Bait

So you got that sexy thing's phone number. Well played. If you just got their e-mail or were told "Find me on Facebook!", sorry. There will be neither Cooking nor Banging for you. Always get their number!

Now you need to lure them to your pad. A first date at your place is unusual so you gotta sell it. Your shiny awesomeness might suffice to get some cutie to trot their buns into your sex lair. But finesse is the key to avoid blowing a month's worth of beer money at a fancy restaurant. If they aren't happy eating an amazing feast prepared in your humble abode, they are gold-diggers not worth your time. Many dates will hesitate about coming over to your pad, especially on a first date. If you're brash enough to invite them over for dinner, you better give them a good reason to come over. For some reason, "all-night-bangathon" doesn't sell.

THE BAIT

Every good trap has bait to lure its prey. The same rules apply to a dinner date. They should enter your trap by their own free will. Sometimes an amazing meal available only in your kitchen is enough for a bona fide foodie or nymphomaniac. But that won't be enough to get the rest to tear through your front door in a hurry. Appeal to their interests and passions. Build this into your game early. Determine what they are enthusiastic about and improvise with something related. Always have something mind-blowing at your place that gets their cerebral panties in a bunch. That could be a piece of art, a cult movie they have never seen, a saltwater aquarium with jellyfish, or Bolivian marching powder you smuggled up your bum.

THE HOOK

The orgasmic meal is the hook that will seal the deal once you lure them over. Cooking and Banging will surely follow. Coming over to your house instead of Bleu Balls Bistro is a rarefied privilege. Work food into the conversation early and keep it up as a central theme. Pay attention to what foods they like so you can surprise them. Be sure to hint that you're a good cook without boasting. You want their mouths watering long before they take their first bite. When all else fails, tell them that you have a recipe that you've been perfecting for years that will change their life.

Luring girls over to my house with food has been my bangable bread and butter. Years ago, I had my eyes on a super cute cupcake chef at one of those fancy boutiques by my office. This cupcake cutie blew off the hordes of men (my co-workers) angling for her nether regions. So I devised a scheme to make me stand out from the pack. I'd present her with one of my own culinary concoctions each day I bought a cupcake. She was intrigued by my antics and accepted my challenge for a bake-off at my place. The bake-off evolved into a clothes-off. She won the contest, I won the prize.

So once you've got your game plan mapped out, how do you lure and then snare your next victim—er, date?

HOLY HOTTIES

You picked up some Holy Hottie at a religious event you attended out of an obligation to your parents. It was some backyard potluck with casseroles and punch. Bored, you chatted up the best-looking person there, ignoring the glaring signs of Jesus on a cross screaming out, "Back off, perv!" You were the wolf in lamb of God's clothing, claiming to love the Lord even more than you love Creed. You kept the conversation light, funny without offending, and demonstrated good Christian life-partner skills. Most importantly, you made an impression that left them tingling with premarital lust. The phone number was yours for the taking. When the time comes, what do you say?

YOU: Hello there, [Holy Hottie]. It's [your name] from the BBQ.

They will most certainly remember because they don't give their number out often.

YOU: It was such a delight talking to you. What a fun party! I didn't realize they made Born-Again Trivial Pursuit. Mrs. Magdalene's casserole was something else, wasn't it?

They'll agree because that's how uber-polite Christians roll. Steer the conversation toward their interests. In this case, it's music.

YOU: Closing out the night singing "Kumbaya" was a perfect nightcap. I just love to sing. Don't you? Not that I'm gay; those guys are going to burn in hell.

They will agree, but you already knew that. With rapport established, transition into inviting them over.

YOU: So I was curious if you have any interest in checking out this rare Creed DVD I have. They're playing live for a crowd of rehabilitated homosexuals. You can literally see Jesus penetrating each one of those blasphemers!

Of course they want to. Holy Hotties are totally gay for Christian rock.

YOU: God bless you! Come over to my place tomorrow night with a hungry tummy and open ears. Pretend you're Moses after forty years in the desert with no food or music.

Nice work, my child. Now I command you to make them scream out the Lord's name in vain.

YUMMY YUPPIES

This time you found yourself at a corporate coffee shop buying yourself a corporate coffee before your interview for a corporate job. Your eyes locked on a perfect ass not quite hidden by a power pantsuit in front of you. You nearly spilled half-and-half at the coffee condom-ment station on their shirt. You apologized, blaming stress—it's a bear market, after all! They relate and are impressed by the job you claim you already have at the company (if they work there, then you just got pwned). After chatting for a few minutes about bullshit acronyms—LIBORS and P&Es and OPPs—you had to run for your important meeting (interview). But you grabbed their digits first so you could "carry on this conversation via BBM." Now it's time to capitalize on your assets (their number).

YOU: Hey, [Yummy Yuppie]. It's [your name] from D-bag Holdings Group.

Yuppies tend to associate people through the companies they work for. So remind them in case their mind is on spreadsheets and corporate retreats.

YOU: We met at Starbucks. I was the klutz who nearly ruined your suit with half-and-half. It would be a shame to have ruined Mr. Dolce & Gabbana's craftsmanship.

Of course. How could they forget? After all, you left quite the impression. They'll tell you about work, so relate to them with business banality.

YOU: I know how that goes. Things have been crazy for me
   with the end of the quarter coming up. Those jacked up interest rates aren't making life any easier. Have they affected
   your company's revenue? Credit default swaps won't clean
   up the toxic assets dripping down my face!

Allow them to hem and haw about their own recent work experiences. Laugh at the right moments and display a sense of
empathy. Ask pointed questions that inspire them to reveal
vulnerabilities you can exploit. Then steer the conversation toward gourmet food, something Yummy Yuppies hold in high
regard.

YOU: Have you been to Café le Prétension? Totally amazing!
   Although their [fancy dish] doesn't hold a candle to the one
   I make. Hey, you should come to my place after work and
   try it.

Chances are, their schedule is crazy and they barely have time to
eat, let alone bang. But considering how stressed Yummy Yuppies are, they need a full release. Be a sport and give it to them.
Chances are they will be using you for sex. Don't sweat the food
too much—when they agree, just go with it!

HIPPIE HARLOTS

You don't usually associate with the hairy ones. But this one Hippie Harlot is cute, young, and naïve. The bitterness about the
revolution passing them by has not yet set in, and they miraculously use deodorant (Tom's of Maine, natch). You picked them
up after a power yoga class where you witnessed their promising
flexibilities. The object now is to not reveal your cynicism be-

cause you are totally Zen, bro. Back at the yoga studio you talked about trendy Eastern religions, spirituality, and your most recent trip to India where you visited an ashram. They bit, and now you've got their number. Time to go tantric!

YOU: [In a super chill, laid-back voice.] Yo, [Hippie Harlot]. It's [your name] from The Booty Tree.

Their brain is coated with bong resin so they may not remember what they ate for lunch. A little reminder nudge always helps.

YOU: We were stretching partners. [Still nothing.] I went to that ashram in India and had an opium colonic.

Nice work. They remembered something that happened less than a week ago. If you waited any longer, your memory would have faded away like Jerry Garcia.

YOU: I want to show you the pictures from all my spiritual journeys. There's India of course, but also some great shots of sacred ceremonies in Machu Picchu and Tibet.

Don't worry if you've never left the country. Pull images from online and import them into your computer's photo organizer. You aren't in any pictures because that is a narcissistic Western practice that you have transcended. Just to sweeten the pot:

YOU: We can make this amazing organic vegan macrobiotic recipe. It's part of my super cleanse. It flushes all those corporate toxins that block your chi.

Your Hippie Harlot will be all about it. Watch them transform into a free lovin' slut. Just don't put a label on it, man. It's just your auras momentarily joining. So open up their chakras and their legs will spread open, too. Peace!

HIPSTER HO-BAGS

This hipster fad has taken to a generation like a case of full body herpes. But you still went to see a friend's band at a warehouse party infested with hipsters. You struggled not to ridicule their outfits and retarded sense of irony. Across the room you saw a Hipster Ho-bag drinking a can of PBR trying to look ugly, but failing. You managed to get past the nonprescription glasses, ill-fitting vintage T-shirt for TEEN ABSTINENCE DAY 1987, and pants tight enough to make you feel claustrophobic by proxy. Underneath that clown suit they call fashion is a smoking hot body just longing to be freed, so you told them how 80s they looked. You both laughed about how your friend's band will get popular, sell out, and then suck. Neither of you will listen then because the music will cease being so bad that it's awesome. You act just bored enough to get their phone number.

YOU: [In a lackadaisical, I don't care if they say *no* mode, grumble.] What's up, [Hipster Ho-bag]? It's [your name] from that super lame warehouse party Saturday.

Hopefully they remember you since they have probably given their number out to half of Williamsburg. Just lay the sarcasm on thick and sigh a lot. Remind them that your friend is in the band you were both mocking.

YOU: I was the one who left just before the headliner came on. Girl Talk is so last month. [Still nothing.] Remember we renamed my friend's shitty band The Carpetbaggers?

The Hipster Ho-bag you're keen to bang remembers now and sounds only quasi-excited to hear from you. Don't take it personally. They haven't been stoked about anything they couldn't snort since the 90s. Make an obscure reference:

YOU: That party was like a nightmare starring Vicki from *Small Wonder*. I mean, where the fuck is Jamie Lawson when you need him?

You have now earned serious brownie points for your knowledge of 80s pop culture. Now they will succumb to your desires.

YOU: So I just went to the Goodwill for a new messenger bag. You have to see this crazy children's book in Braille I picked up. It's decker than shit!

Your suggestion sounds outlandish enough for them to brag about it later so they agree.

YOU: We can totally eat homemade empanadas, drink PBR, and read in Braille.

Translation: You will bang them senseless while maintaining a look of complete indifference.

CLUB SLUTS AND DANCE FLOOR D-BAGS

You met at a noisy club. They shook their ass while sipping an apple martini at a nearby VIP table. You pretended to know "Dave" so you could sidle up next to them and comment on how you saw the DJ once in Ibiza. They're impressed, but you learned your new friend is not terribly bright. But their ass looked great in that sparkly getup so you get the phone number and retreat before Dave exposes you as a fraud. Now it's time to call.

YOU: Hey [Club Slut/Dance Floor D-bag]. It's [your name].

If they don't remember, remind them.

YOU: You know, [your name], we met at Bridge and Tunnel. I was with Dave's birthday party.

They vaguely remember, but the drinks, drugs, and dancing have eroded their brain. (This bodes well for a rocking one-night stand.)

YOU: I really loved that sparkly miniskirt/muscle shirt you were wearing. I'm surprised you weren't arrested for public indecency.

They laugh, which means you're in.

YOU: So I'm going to the opening of Club Wank and have a plus one. Interested?

They will be so stoked, your deal is already sealed. But don't worry if you aren't Mr. Saturday Night on the club scene. If you Cook to Bang, you won't have to worry about later that night.

YOU: Come over to my pad first and we'll get our pre-party on. I'll make some tapas I learned to make during my last Ibiza trip. We can listen to my latest [British pronunciation] garage-reggaeton mashup.

Don't worry if you're not a DJ or that they probably won't eat much, if at all. They'll come over and drink plenty. Rock the Cook to Bang method and start a techno dance party in their pants.

SORORITEASES AND FRAT-HOLES

Man, that Eta Pi party was off the hizzy, yo! The *Girls Gone Wild* camera crew filmed those Sororiteases grinding against the entire football team and kissing each other. It was a low-IQ paradise. You aren't technically in the frat or even going to the college. But fuck it. Free booze and slutty girls. Your classic Frat-hole-inspired pump-and-grind dance got Daddy's little whore to wipe her ass sweat all over your jeans—in a good way. The natives realized you didn't belong and tried to throw you out on your ass. But on the way out you nimbly grabbed another beer and the skank's number signed with an *XO* after their name.

YOU: [Be boorish and misogynistic.] Whaddup, [Sororitease/ Frat-hole]? It's [your name] from that Eta Pi-hole rager.

Chances are they were too sauced on roofie coladas to remember how well acquainted you became with their backside. Be specific, or just make shit up. They are in their bad girl/boy phase before they go establishment anyway.

YOU: Yeah. Those Eta Pi boys sure know how to throw down. Were you there when they made their pledges give that dog head?

Even if your new friend wasn't there, they will claim they were. Being in the Greek system is all about belonging. Exploit that.

YOU: What kind of crazy shit does [their sorority/frat] get into? I heard you guys get retarded once the boxed wine starts flowing.

Allow them to tell wild stories of girl-on-girl action, body shots, and public indecency. They will snicker about it behind their future spouse's back years from now. Now it's time to make a cameo in their sordid little secrets.

YOU: You're a great dancer! Sorry your friends dragged you away when you blacked out. Did a pledge roofie you? I'll kick their ass. You know I can bench like three hundred?

They are sufficiently impressed with your superficial qualities, so close in for the kill.

YOU: So I'm trying to make these wings for the tailgate this weekend. Wanna come over and taste test?

Most Greeks are WAY into school team camaraderie since they are athletes or bang them. Besides, they are exorcising their slutty demons before joining the Republican party. Join the hallowed halls of the youthful indiscretions they will fantasize about when they are being carelessly banged by their bored spouse.

NASCAR NASTIES

Your NASCAR-loving amigo scored pit seats for the local smash 'em up speedway series. You wanted to understand the sport more popular than football, basketball and baseball combined. The engines roared, the people cheered, but you couldn't tear your eyes off the smoking hot motor oil spokesmodel. They looked bored too so you sidled up next to them between fake smiles and insincere waves. Your new friend enjoyed your antics and told you about their white trash dream to become a professional cheerleader. *Genius* wouldn't be the first word to describe them, but they knew enough to remember their phone number. Fortunately, it's not her/his personality you want to delve deeper into.

YOU: Hey, y'all [no need for name]. It's [your name] from the Houston 500. The one with all his/her teeth.

Remind them that you aren't the typical beer-guzzling race fan propositioning them to get freaky in your trailer. Talk a little NASCAR shop from talking points you researched online.

YOU: Did you watch the Trash & Smash 'Em Up 700? Can you believe Jeff Gordon and Dale Jr.? That crash was worse than when I rammed Daddy's tractor into the barn. Hoo-wee!

Your NASCAR Nasty will go on and on about how cute so-and-so who races for what-and-what is. Listen, comment when appropriate, and give them time to gab on, thus arming you with manipulation ammunition. Invite them over when they stop yapping.

YOU: I have a bunch of classic racing moments on DVD. [Rent it.] Some of the best finishes, passes, and crashes. Let's watch 'em and eat my world famous Who da Mac & Cheese.

They will be flattered. They are used to going on dates to Hooters or the Cracker Barrel. Serve some delicious "real people" food while watching cars go *vroom vroom* until y'all go boom boom.

9

Pregame to Bang

Now that your date's set up, optimize your prospects. Setting the mood is essential to the art of culinary seduction. Don't expect your date to walk through your front door, take one bite of a microwaved meal, and assume the position. Remember: the reason you didn't call a whore is because you are too goddamn cheap.

When it comes to a dinner date, pregaming is essential. Think of it like prepping to go out, but the two of you are going nowhere but your bedroom. Remove any snags that could trip up your game. Don't overlook minor details. A used condom wrapper can condemn your Herculean efforts. That's game over no matter what you cook, what drinks you pair with the food, or the connection you build. You will find yourself doing the dishes early and desperately texting booty calls of last resort.

You want the polar opposite: for them to insist on satisfying your every urge. That requires comfort. No one is going to put out unless they are at ease (unless you pay them—see above). This should not be some random trollop you ravaged in the photo booth at the back of the bar. This date is classy and presumably out of your league. You will blow their mind with the simple, effective Cook to Bang method. So sweat the details.

Stack the chips in your favor. Play to win. COOK TO FUCK-ING BANG!

LIGHT TO BANG

Visual impressions stay in our mind long after the smell of lust fades away. That's why the lights in your pad need to be your wingmen, not a kick in the nuts. Illuminate your libido with lights that make your guest go "Oh fucking yes!" instead of "Hell fucking no!"

Candles

Candlelit dinners are cliché, but flickering light is hypnotic. It's man's primitive worship of fire. You become Prometheus stealing the flame from Mount Olympus. The drawback is candles are obvious and can appear try-hard. The best approach is to have the candles on the dinner table already, which is only fitting if you Cook to Bang often. Don't appear to be pulling out all stops to impress them (even if you are). Use candles in candleholders. Don't cheap out with those one-dollar glass Jesus candles (unless your date is a Hipster Ho-bag). You don't want your date thinking you still live in your mom's basement.

Softer Is Better

Soft lighting is essential. Flickering fluorescent lights belong in a doctor's waiting room. Unless you are playing doctor, or are a doctor, don't let your date's mind wander to their last pap smear or prostate exam. Soft light is sexier. Having blemishes or being a deformed man-thing becomes less obvious. The only place bright lights make sense is in the kitchen. Your cooking corner doesn't need to be lit up like a porn shoot, but you should be able to see so you don't set your pad or date on fire. Allow for a smoother transition to the dinner table where soft light is essential for creating intimacy. You never want to alter the lighting blatantly. Your intentions and next move will become predictable. Keep the lights at a constant level of sexy and make like a seduction ninja. Your date shouldn't realize what's up until your tongue is already in their mouth.

Lighting That Works

Be smart when you shop for your lighting. The cooler the lights you buy, the better off your libido. Antiques are winners so long as they aren't a fire hazard or clash with the rest of your furniture. Offbeat lamps are also great so long as they don't make you look like an overgrown teenager. I have a ridiculous lamp that rotates with dolphins and fish swimming. I call it my ocean view and it always gets a laugh.

Passion-Igniting Lighting	Cock-Blocking Lighting
Lamps (art or antique)	Overhead lights
Overhead lights with dimmers	Lava lamp
Candles	Desk lamp
Rope lights	Spotlight
Christmas lights	TV on mute

CLEAN YOUR SHIT UP!

Good hygiene can make the difference between getting off and getting online to download porn. That means cleaning your place before your date arrives. How old are you anyway? Take a little pride in your personal space. At least appear to have your shit together. Don't let them think that your sex lair doubles as a frat house. Cockroaches crawling out of the pizza

box tower in your living room doesn't scream hot sex on a platter. A gross pad will create discomfort and yield no banging.
You don't have to be a germaphobe in a Hazmat suit. Just wipe
down the nasty once in a while.

YOUR LIVING ROOM

Chances are you will first hook up with your date in the living
room. You will be chilling on the couch after the impressive
meal you made. Don't screw the pooch by being careless. Keep
the place free of excuses for your date to change their mind.

Frame Something

Kids have posters hung with thumbtacks. Adults have framed
posters or art. This speaks volumes for you, so get with the
program!

Make It Sparkle

Keeping your living room spotless is essential because it is here
where your date decides how far they will let you get with them.

Hide Anything Offensive

That means porno mags, loaded guns, or your laptop open to
cooktobang.com.

Remove All Paraphernalia

Unless your date partakes in your vices, it's best to keep the
bongs, syringes, and crack pipes hidden.

YOUR BATHROOM

So many supposedly mature people just don't get it. Your date
will use your bathroom at some point if things go well. Keep it

hygienic. You don't need a maid to keep your date from running away in terror. Here are some bathroom basics you should already know.

Clean the Toilet

You don't want questionable substances caked to the bowl or floating menacingly on top.

Keep Toilet Paper Stocked

Newsflash, guys. Girls use a lot of toilet paper. Don't make them call out desperately to you for a new roll. Let them maintain their feminine mystique . . . before you violate it, that is.

Wipe Down the Sink and Counter

All it takes is a wet cloth or paper towel. Ten seconds of your time to remove the scum, you scumbag.

Hang Your Towels Neatly

This is another simple move. Seduction is all about details.

YOUR BEDROOM

This is where the good times roll in the hay, the date's final destination. Don't shoot your game in the crotch when you make it this far.

Wash Those Sheets

You don't want cum stains or pubes exposing your past indiscretions.

Make Your Bed

That doesn't mean a fancy hotel tuck you will undo in the throes of passion. It's just sexier to fall into a made bed than one that is unkempt, dirty, and covered with stank-ass gym clothes.

Pick Up Your Crap

Don't leave a massive pile of clothes in the middle of the floor. Buy a hamper or just stuff them into your closet or deep under your bed.

Destroy All Evidence

Always remove evidence of previous playtime pals such as jewelry, lingerie, hair clips, anal beads, etc. Never ever leave used condoms in the trash!

YOURSELF

There's a reason why hippies usually date other hippies. It's a hygiene thing. The rest of our noses have standards. We don't want to hook up with Granola Girl or the Grizzly Man. So clean your body before a date.

Wash Away the Sin

You don't want to reek of anything but sex appeal.

A Clean Shave

Unless you're rocking some hipster 'stache, shave before a date. Ladies, this should be obvious. Chin burn and chafed legs after monkey sex aren't pleasant.

To Smell or Not to Smell

Whether that means deodorant, cologne, perfume, or au naturel, you want to smell good, but subtle. Overpowering scents are worse than BO.

Makeup or Break Up

Ladies: doing yourself up before a date never hurt nobody. Accentuate your beauty. Guys: the eyeliner is not necessary!

AROMATHERAPY

The olfactory senses are the most sensitive to stimulation and revulsion. The nose knows if you will remove those pantyhose. The solution is to keep things smelling pleasant, not putrid. That means showering with soap. Back when I was a smelly longhair in college, I thought a rinse off would suffice. I was wrong. The same rules apply to your pad.

Make a great olfactory first impression by being halfway through the cooking when your date arrives. Their sensual scent memories will trigger. In the back of their mind they will think, "Keeper." This puts you in control. You are cooking anyway, so start it off right. It can't be obvious that you've been waiting for them with bated breath with your hands down your pants. Also, the smell of good food can negate rancid smells you couldn't quite hide.

Makes Scents	Non-Scents
Tantalizing food	Excess incense or oils
Fresh flowers (in a vase, not bag)	Rancid refrigerator (clean it)
Scented candles	Stinky trash (take it out)
Cologne/perfume (don't overdo it)	Cat piss/shit (clean the litter box)
Clean pet (use to your advantage)	Disinfectant (disguising something worse)

NO INTERRUPTIONS

Cook to Bang can't happen with an audience unless your date is an exhibitionist. Wooing requires that no interference derail the connection. Get your pad all to yourself. If you live alone, lucky you! Single people who live alone always fare better. You don't owe anyone an explanation or apology. (Just don't get your dates mixed up and invite them over the same night, unless you're sure you can pull off a threesome.) Most young singles have roommates or live with their family out of necessity. You may love and adore the people you live with, but know that they are game killers.

Roommates

Young adults live with a friend or acquaintance because they haven't quite made it. These can be nurturing friendships. But sharing your pad isn't conducive to Cooking and Banging. You can't seduce with your oblivious roommate watching *Sports Center* in their underwear. If your roomie likes to party, they might bring the whole bar home. And worst of all, they may try stealing your date. So what's a Cook to Banger to do?

ROOMMATE CONTINGENCY PLAN

Plan Date Around Roomie's Work Schedule
You'll know they aren't home.

Keep Roommate Informed
They should not come back without warning.

Devise Communication System
Just like in college: rubber band on doorknob.

Beg Them to Vanish
You will owe them a favor, like doing the dishes for a week.

Make Them Camp Out in Their Room
Have them hide out like Anne Frank while you CTB.

Family

First off, my apologies if you live at home. That's player's kryptonite. Worry not, for someday you can afford to live in your own den of debauchery. For now, your moments free from parents, grandparents, and siblings are rare. Chances are you will be interrupted by an annoying sibling singing "[your name] and [date's name] sitting in a tree." Innovation is the bastard child of inconvenience. I have faith that you will spin the situation into a less pathetic hue.

HOW TO CTB LIVING WITH YOUR FOLKS

Bribe Siblings to Fuck Off
You never want to hear taunting while macking.

Host When They Leave Town
Only interruption will be from a home invasion.

Early to Bed Early to Rise
While your folks are sleeping, you are freaking.

Reignite the Romance
Tell your parents they deserve a night out together.

Double Date with Your Folks
Just slam your nuts in a drawer. Much less painful.

THE DINNER TABLE

Do yourself a favor. Get a dining room table with matching chairs. Your mojo depends on it. Besides, you aren't blowing serious coin at a restaurant. Never make cooking at home seem like the shortcut that it is. Always eat at a table when you Cook to Bang, unless you only serve appetizers and wine. That's how grown-ups eat. Your dates will be more responsive if you don't plop your asses on the couch with plates in your laps. Here's why:

Eye contact: Conversation will flow like a waterfall.
Better digestion: Indigestion from slouching = fail.
Behold, your feast: Spread out your culinary triumph.
Banging on the table: Sweep everything off and ravage your date.

Set the Table

That extra mile spent setting the table is well worth it. Don't be the bozo that places everything in the wrong place. Would you pitch a tent haphazardly, setting poles up according to your laziest whim? Of course not! The tent would come crashing down at the slightest breeze or chupacrabra attack. Why set up the frame for your meal with any less care? Place the right utensils in the right locations. Make sure they match. Don't serve wine in a vintage *E.T.* glass or *Back to the Future* thermos. There are essential table-setting laws.

Oh yes!

Hell no!

Glasses

1. You need separate wine- and water glasses.
2. Keep them full at all times.
3. The glasses sit above and to the right of the plate from left to right: water, red wine, white wine, dessert wine (when your butler Winston is on duty).

Silverware

1. Plastic utensils are only appropriate for picnics or NASCAR Nasties.
2. Forks go on the left in this order: dinner fork on the inside, salad fork on the outside (to the left of the dinner fork, Beavis).
3. The knife and spoon go on the right, Butthead.

Plates

1. The dinner plate goes right in front of you.
2. The bread plate goes above and to the left of the dinner plate.

Napkins

1. Use clean, matching cloth napkins. Save the paper towels for pizza with the bros.
2. Napkins always go to the left of the plate.

3. Wrap your silverware in the napkins, or use them as blindfolds. Or origami orgy time: stuff a napkin in a glass like a fan or wrap it into a rose.

MUSIC SELECTION

Everyone has his or her own musical tastes. While some songs make you cream your pants, other songs make you prefer to hear the death rattle of your only child. It speaks volumes for our over-privileged and self-indulgent culture that we have the luxury to debate it ad nauseam. Entire social cliques are built around musical tastes. Beatniks, hippies, punks, hip-hoppers, grunge rockers, ravers, hipsters, and whatever comes next all have a soundtrack to their lives. And we haven't touched on subgenres.

My conundrum is that the hottest women listen to the worst music. Ever been to a trendy club with the most beautiful people? I'm picky about my music and Top 40 inspires me to lie down in traffic. Sometimes I just swallow my pride and pretend to enjoy it for the sake of my libido. Still it's best to figure out what music your date digs either by asking them directly or investigating like a Digital Dick, as we discussed in chapter 3. Your best bet is to shelve your obscure grooves unless your date shares your love for Tuvan throat singers.

That doesn't mean you can't turn them on . . . to something new. Tread lightly with the mainstream dates like Yummy Yuppies and Sororiteases/Frat-holes. Their ears are less receptive to music unavailable in the Walmart music aisle. Play something in line with their tastes that is less abrasive to your ears. You want to be able to open up their world to all sorts of experiences. Just be sure the unfamiliar music doesn't sound like monks disemboweling each other. That double live album of "My Shiny Small Intestine" isn't date soundtrack material.

The clever Cook to Bang chef has music prepped before their date arrives. Technology leaves you with no excuse for not prepping the perfect seduction mix. Make a mix tape if you still live in the 80s. There's always your computer, iPod, or other mp3 device. You don't want to fumble around in the midst of macking to find that one song by that one band on that one album.

> ## ¡NO *TENGO* HARD-ON!
> Ever find yourself getting down listening to a sexy tune when suddenly the next track murders the vibe? I have. Right as I was about to boldly go where many have gone before, I heard my Spanish language lessons. *"!Hola! Soy Juan. ¡Donde esta el banco?"* My wood fell faster than you can yell, "Timber!"

Sexy music is in the ear of the beholder. But I have compiled a list of music that has led to both my success stories and humiliating failures. No doubt, some of you will dismiss my suggestions as pure poppycock. What do I know about music anyway? My expertise lies in cooking and banging.

Genres to Make 'Em Holler	Genres that Cause Epic Fails
Jazz and blues	Death metal
Down tempo beats	Religious music
World music	Red state country
Classic rock	Stand-up comedy
Hip-hop	Foreign language lessons

Cook to Bang Certified Sexy Time Albums
- Belle and Sebastian—*If You're Feeling Sinister*
- Blur—*Parklife*
- Boards of Canada—*Music Has the Right to Children*

- The Brian Jonestown Massacre—*Tepid Peppermint Wonderland*
- Leonard Cohen—*The Best of Leonard Cohen*
- Miles Davis—*Kind of Blue*
- Depeche Mode—*Violator*
- DJ Shadow—*Endtroducing*
- Duke Ellington—*The OKeh Ellington*
- Fischerspooner—*#1*
- Fleetwood Mac—*Rumours*
- *The Good, the Bad & the Queen*
- Al Green—*Greatest Hits*
- Groove Armada—*Vertigo*
- Jimi Hendrix—*Electric Ladyland*
- Hot Chip—*The Warning*
- Kraftwerk—*Trans-Europe Express*
- Kruder & Dorfmeister—*The K&D Sessions*
- Fela Kuti—*Zombie*
- *LCD Soundsystem*
- Manu Chao—*La Radiolina*
- Massive Attack—*Mezzanine*
- Curtis Mayfield—*Superfly* soundtrack
- MC Solaar—*Paradisiaque*
- Medeski Martin & Wood—*Shack Man*
- MGMT—*Oracular Spectacular*
- Morcheeba—*Who Can You Trust?*
- Mos Def—*Black on Both Sides*
- Prince—*Purple Rain*
- Radiohead—*Kid A*
- RJD2—*Deadringer*
- Nina Simone—*My Baby Just Cares for Me*
- Pink Floyd—*Wish You Were Here*

- Portishead—*Roseland NYC Live*
- Puccini—*Tosca*
- Tribe Called Quest—*Midnight Marauders*
- Tricky—*Maxinquaye*
- Ulrich Schnauss—*Far Away Trains Passing By*
- The Velvet Underground—*Live at Max's Kansas City*
- The White Stripes—*Elephant*
- Zero 7—*Simple Things*

Cook to Bang Me Now Playlist
- Air—"Highschool Lover"
- The Beastie Boys—"Hey Ladies"
- Beck—"Debra"
- Belle and Sebastian—"Stars of Track and Field"
- Boards of Canada—"Olson"
- Blur—"Jets"
- The Brian Jonestown Massacre—"Anenome"
- Manu Chao—"King of the Bongo"
- The Chemical Brothers—"Get Yourself High"
- Cornelius—"Tone Twilight Zone"
- Depeche Mode—"Enjoy the Silence"
- Diggable Planets—"Rebirth of Slick (Cool Like Dat)"
- Electric Six (with Jack White)—"Danger! High Voltage"
- Ella Fitzgerald and Louis Armstrong—"La Vie en Rose"
- Fatboy Slim—"The Weekend Starts Here"
- Fischerspooner—"Emerge"
- The Good, the Bad & the Queen—"History Song"
- Groove Armada—"At the River"
- Chris Isaak—"Wicked Game"
- Jane's Addiction—"Summertime Rolls"
- Kid Koala—"Drunk Trumpet"

- Kraftwerk—"Autobahn"
- Kruder & Dorfmeister—"Original Bedroom Rockers"
- LCD Soundsytem—"Disco Infiltrator"
- Peggy Lee—"Fever"
- Morcheeba—"Moog Island"
- Mos Def—"Ms. Fat Booty"
- Portishead—"Only You"
- Prince—"Darling Nikki"
- Radiohead—"Nude"
- RJD2—"Smoke & Mirrors"
- Nina Simone—"My Baby Just Cares for Me"
- Tosca—"Worksong"
- Tricky—"Hell Is Round the Corner"
- Ulrich Schnauss—"Knuddelmaus"
- The Velvet Underground—"Pale Blue Eyes"
- The White Stripes—"You've Got Her in Your Pocket"
- Zero 7—"In the Waiting Line"

Mood Murdering Music

- Dane Cook—Anywhere you hear his voice
- Billy Ray Cyrus—"Achy Breaky Heart"
- Kenny G—*Breathless*
- Gwar—*Scumdogs of the Universe*
- Diana Krall—*When I Look in Your Eyes*
- Barry Manilow—*Ultimate Manilow*
- Raffi—*Greatest Hits*
- *Rent!*—musical soundtrack
- Whale mating songs
- Yanni—*Live at Acropolis*

10

Vibe to Bang

Cooking to Bang yields solid results. Just ask the team of astrophysicists I hired with my billion-dollar Cook to Bang grant. We tested the CTB theory using the super collider as an oven and caused all the female lab assistants to climax simultaneously.

Cooking for a date is self-lubricating foreplay. This begs the question: "What must you do while you Cook in order to Bang?" Create the vibe. Duh!

Delicate orchestration is the variable that determines how successful your culinary seduction shall be. Be nonchalant as you guide the chips to fall into place. Banging should seem like the last thing on your mind. A hookup should never seem contrived. It will end with an awkward kiss and an excuse about waking up early for a lobotomy. The best-laid plans will ring hollow, and your manipulation will be exposed. Let the night unfold naturally and remember that your mojo is the unwavering constant of this kinky equation. Below are methods to employ to harness that carnal connection.

EYES ON THE PRIZE

Didn't your parents ever teach you to look someone in the eye when you communicate? You can't command their respect without giving some in return. If you can't hold their gaze, how can you expect to gaze upon their naked body? So much is communicated through the eyes. I always know if someone is being genuine or a lying sack of shit by looking into their eyes. Those who don't look you in the eye don't respect you, are planning to fuck you over, or both.

The eyes are your window into their soul. Those souls need to connect before they can bang. Hopefully the soul you are trying to enter is corruptable and up for some tarnishing. You can't enter if the blinds are drawn. Holding someone's gaze exudes confidence and strength. Your date won't bang a girlieman or sketchy skank who can't look them in the eye. Keep the vibe going with that simple step.

Attention male readers: Your eyes should never drift down to your date's cleavage for more than a second. Never ogle, no matter how luscious those fun bags maybe. Countless female friends have told me they've blown off dates they would have banged if they hadn't been so transfixed on their mammary glands. There will be plenty of time for motorboating if you Cook to Bang like a champ. Keep ogling if you prefer jerking off to climbing those magic mountains. To my female readers: Checking your watch or phone during a date is just as much of a turnoff. You can't expect some guy to respect you if you don't show them respect.

SMILE, IT'S FREE

I presume you have seen a dentist at some point in your life. Show those chompers off! Even your pearly off-whites can't be as unsightly as a grimace or scowl. The only way that your date will enjoy themselves and relax is if you lead by example. That means smile, sucker! If you plan to convince your date to lie down with you, you best turn that frown upside down. So what if you are on some blind date you reluctantly agreed to to appease your mother, friend, or boss? If that's the case, crocodile smile and sport-fuck them for practice. Keep your game and libido limber for when it counts.

Did you know that smiling is infectious? It's more contagious than ebola and almost as sexy. A smile can sway even the crabbiest date over from the sexually repressed dark side. They will have no choice but to remove the tyrannical stick up their ass when you are so goddamn pleasant. But you're in rough waters when your date doesn't smile back. They may be having a bad day because they stubbed a toe, were denied promotion, or failed to score Radiohead tickets. That shouldn't discourage you from being a ray of sunshine that lights up the room. Your date will shine from your reflective glory.

Should pleasantry fail, you are dealing with a cold fish. At least you know not to make a move on an emotional corpse. Chances are the only pleasure this Debbie Downer or Douglas D-bag enjoys comes from kicking puppies. Get them out of your place as soon as possible. Save that dessert you made for one of your fuck buddies who appreciates your cooking and banging skills.

FULL-BODY CONTACT

For the record, I'm not talking about turning your date into a game of rugby. Granted, the rugby club at my college was just an excuse for Goldschläger orgies. I'm talking about maintaining subtle physical throughout the date. That doesn't mean sticking your tongue down your date's throat when they walk through the door. If you can pull that off, you don't need this book. I presume you'll more likely receive a kicking, rather than a caressing, of your groin. The type of contact I speak of is of the subtle variety that continues throughout the evening, from the hello hug to the kiss goodbye after breakfast.

The object is to get your date used to your touch. Break down those physical boundaries without seeming like you're trying. They will only resist your first move if it's awkward or abrupt. It's like boiling a frog slowly. Toss the croaker in boiling water and it will hop the fuck out. Start if off in tepid water and the frog will think it's a hot tub party. At a certain point it will be too late for them to resist.

The best contact is friendly and nonaggressive, like it's no big deal. There are plenty of opportunities throughout the course of cooking and eating for you to touch your date.

Subtle Contact Moves	
High-five	Footsie while you eat
Fist bump	Rub elbows while cooking
Caress lower back	Scratch their back
Shoulder rub	Crack their back
Play with their hair	Hold hands
Lean in to examine jewelry	Read their palm

SHUT YOUR MOUTH AND OPEN YOUR EARS

The most popular conversation subject for most humans is themselves. Every first date I've been on was a volley of autobiographical monologues. Vagina Monologues, Penis Soliloquies, it's basically the same shit. It's a spattering of "I grew up there," "I went to this school there," and "I work here." Most people's lives are goddamn boring. There's a reason why television is most people's BFF.

Keep the spotlight on your dinner companion. Never dominate the conversation; you'll come off as an egomaniac. Nothing you have to say is change-the-world important to warrant rambling like a flippant dick. Don't lay out your top five accomplishments in the first five minutes. Pace yourself when passing out the breadcrumbs of your fascinating life. The fact you won a Peabody Award for best oral sex video tutorial can wait . . . until dessert. Speak less, but say more. You want them hanging on your every word. Leave some room for mystery and never incriminate yourself. There's no fifth amendment in dating. I've heard more than one girl say of her date, "I thought he was so hot until he opened his mouth."

Shut the fuck up and listen with extreme prejudice. Your date is more likely to sleep with you if you let them ramble on.

This is especially true of women who discuss their dreams, aspirations, and shopping splurge for hours without taking a breath. Rather than add to the noise pollution, let your date spew out insider-trading info you can exploit to get in their pants. Ask them pointed questions that get them going on about their first threesome or the time they competed in an amateur stripping contest. Catalog the details for future reference. You free up a lot of brainpower to plot your seduction when you aren't thinking up the next clever thing to say. Now you have ammo to tease them mercilessly with.

FLIRT TO BANG

Flirting is the linchpin of seduction. Create a playful back and forth with your date. It's a two-way street of teasing that draws you together like naughty refrigerator magnets. This is the Teaser Tractor Beam. Increase the intensity of your mutual attraction by keeping them on their toes. Challenge them and be challenged. Much of it is posturing, but ultimately you both get something out of it—besides banging each other's brains out, that is.

The fact that you are a scoundrel becomes irrelevant after you bang. Keep it on the DL until then. You must know where to draw the distinction between flirtation and sleazy cum-ons. Keep the conversation light and full of sexual innuendo, but avoid the perv-in-the-bushes vibe. You can talk about sex, but never mention sex with them directly. It may seem like a good idea to slap your genitals on the table after a glass of wine, but save that for the second date.

Tease them about trivial stuff like the fact they were in a glee club or a sorority/frat. Lay off the heavy subjects about dead grandmothers and physical deficiencies. Keep the tone funny and playful. Razz their asses without alienating or pissing them off. Simple, right?

BE FUNNY, CLOWN

You would be a fool to underestimate how much chemistry lies in humor. There's a reason why pint-size mensches like Woody Allen and David Spade attract the hottest women on the planet. Make them laugh and you will make them moan. No one's going to bang you if they don't enjoy your company (unless their pimp is waiting outside in his emerald-green Cadillac). Keep the giggles coming with your best jokes, stories, and anecdotes. Bonus points if they relate to cooking and food.

In a group of dudes, the funny guy gets the phone number. Beer guts, receding hairlines, and empty bank accounts become nonissues if you are entertaining. Make your date feel like they are watching a standup routine for an audience of one. I have banged my share of "out of my league" girls just by being the funny guy who can cook. My family and friends scratch their heads over how I date hotties with my average looks, height, and income.

Humor leaves a lingering impression. Don't be forgettable by holding back. If they can't handle your flavor, they aren't right for you. I can't date anyone who doesn't find the word *pantsuit* funny. Total deal breaker. So be your most animated self. Don't keep the funny snake in its cage.

KEEP DRINKS FLOWING

Always be a good host. Be ever mindful of your guest's comfort level without hovering. That means keeping their glass full, their mind entertained, and their desires piqued. It's a privilege to drink with you. Don't cheap out with just one bottle of wine or only two beers. Remember the proverb: It's better to have and not want, than need and not have. Make like a good Boy or Girl Scout and be prepared so they stick around to bang you later.

This doesn't mean get your date wasted so you can take advantage of them. That is only appropriate if you are both wasted and mutually taking advantage of each other. A little libation lubrication never hurt nobody. Just don't turn it into a Lifetime movie. Surely no one smart enough to Cook to Bang would rely on such low-rent tactics. Yakking in the sink because the toilet was too far away sends sex appeal out the nearest window.

Your game should be strong enough that you don't need booze as an excuse to make a mistake. It's more about the taste than the buzz anyway, right? Just maintain a comfortable drunken haze that wears off by 3 A.M. when they finally leave.

DANCE WHILE YOU COOK

There is little difference between dancing and banging. Clothing mostly. Two bodies moving in sync to music, eyes locked, in a passionate embrace. The rhythm takes control and releases the dancers from all liability. Blame the music for the escalation of the dance from the kitchen to the bedroom. Sounds like a happy ending.

Great dancers are greater lovers. Your prowess is revealed by the way you move. Keep it goofy and carefree. No harm in two unfamiliar bodies pressing together in the name of dance. You maintain physical contact that will smooth your way into your first kiss. They won't be taken aback if you've already thrown them around the room like a ballroom dancer. You could even steal the first kiss before dinner if you dance with some boy band moves.

There are moments waiting for something to steam, bake, or broil when your busy body opens to the extracurricular. This is the time to be spontaneous. Spin your date around the room while the pasta boils. Let the music playing in the background inspire you to interpretive dance with your giggling date.

HAND-FEED YOUR DATE

You're not at the zoo. It's okay to feed the animals. Just don't overfeed them or throw feces. Hand-feeding someone creates intimacy. Surely it's a sex-slave-feeding-you-grapes thing. Oral stimulation, if you will.

The best way to orally stimulate your date is by keeping them engaged in the culinary process. Make them feel empowered by seeking their input on flavor. Get them emotionally invested in the meal so they become physically invested in you later. Does it need some salt, less seasoning, or more umph? The only way to engage their taste buds is by feeding them. Have them lick your spoon or better yet, your finger. They should be comfortable having your things in their mouth.

What to Put in Your Date's Mouth

Any sauce (with spoon)	Homemade salad dressing (with finger)
Slice of cheese	Your secret rub recipe
Slice of fruit/vegetable	
Any berry, especially strawberries	Cookie or brownie dough
Cake frosting	Grapes, obviously

11

From Cook to Bang

All your Cook to Bang efforts come down to this. Your strategy, approach, menu, drinks, pregaming, flirting, and manipulating all lead you to this moment. It's when your id takes over and pounces. How do you transition from munching food to carpet?

Read the vibe and harness the chemistry. Easier said than done. You can misread signals and end up feeling like a chump. Exposing yourself at the dinner table on the first date may indicate you were a bit cocky. But there is never shame in trying. I have faith that you will guide them like an air traffic controller safely onto your bed. Go from zero to banging in sixty minutes without hitting any cock-blocking red lights. *Vroom* fucking *vroom*!

BECOME BILINGUAL: READ BODY LANGUAGE

You can tell whether the evening will leave you balls deep or balls blue by how your date greets you. A hug or kiss on the cheek is a good omen. A handshake or no contact at all means you'll be spooning your pillow . . . if you're lucky. Humans reveal a lot unwittingly. It's like poker. Be on the lookout for tells (signs) that they are bluffing (being prude) or holding a straight flush (condom in pocket). You will know when it's time to go all in with your pride and transition from Cook to Bang.

You can bluff your way into fornication with enough bravado. That is where your body language comes into play. You can gauge your prospects by their reciprocation. Those who play along, grab back, or smile when you touch them are good to go. If they inch away from you like swine flu is oozing from your pores, you best hide your wounded paw, slow down, and formulate Plan B.

BODY LANGUAGE CHEAT SHEET

Posture

Relaxed and comfy: Banging prospects are good.
Rigid back and shoulders: Your advances will crash and burn.

Eye Contact

If they hold your gaze: You are already banging them with your eyes.
Looking everywhere but at you: Give your eyes a cold shower.

Hair

Playing with their hair: You are making them anxious, aka horny.
Short hair: If they have no locks, watch for fidgeting and twiddling.

Phone Play

Ignoring phone calls on date: They are into you. No banging interference.

Text-messaging throughout date: Booty call with someone else. Check please!

Leaning

Toward you: They are waiting, hoping, and inviting you to pounce.

Away from you: Either it's your BO or crap game. Move on, player.

Position of Knees

Their knees touching yours: From knees knocking to boots knocking.

Their knees drawn far away: You better get their coat.

Smile

Ear-to-ear grin: You should have made your move five minutes ago.

Crocodile smile: Worse than a frown. Chances are they are calculating how to drop you like a hot potato covered in spikes and rigged to blow.

Hands Across the World

Expressive jazz hands: Let them conduct a symphony of ecstasy.

Clenched fists in lap: Repressed hand movements = repressed hip movements.

CHITCHAT

As mentioned in the last chapter, never dominate the conversation or be a pompous gasbag. Let your date yap on about shoes while expertly guiding the conversation toward more favorable subjects. Avoid controversial topics that lure out the liberal or conservative crackpots. Keep it light, fun, and flirty. Dates are supposed to be led to spontaneous NSA (no strings attached) banging, not a poorly written romantic comedy moment.

Whatever you do, never ever EVER bring up the ex, yours or theirs. Cook to Bang isn't about stirring up the ghosts of relationships past. This is doubly true if you both know this person. You become an insensitive anus brain. You might inspire your date to reignite their toxic affair. Why feed the vibe worm-infested meat? You will come off as petty, pathetic, and dwelling on the past. Some respond to the wounded animal vibe, but they usually become more like mother or father figures than sex partners. If conversation derails, guide the sexy train back onto the tracks.

CONVERSATION TOPICS

Oh Yes!	No-nos!
Sexual innuendo	Abortion (be pro-banging)
Food	Religion (WWJD? Shut up!)
Travel	Politics (your candidate lost)
Education	Money (unless it's a gold-digger)
Job you love	
Styles and trends	Job you hate (Kinko's is hiring)
Arts and music	Friends they don't know (who?)
TV and movies	The ex (don't show scrapbook)
Friends in common	Techy shit (your PDA, blah blah)
	Relationships (especially marriage)

PROXIMITY = DEBAUCHERY

Maintain close proximity to your date throughout the evening. The objective is to move ever closer as you flirt, caress, and charm your way into their personal space. Think of it like positioning in business: smack that bottom line's ass. Never cross the line from keen to creepy. You want the transition from talking to kissing to be natural. Don't cross the room to pounce like a lion. Make like a leopard that's already next to them.

Initiate a close proximity as soon as you greet them. Draw closer while you cook, eat, and finally connect. Lean in when you talk, scoot your chair closer so you can "hear them better," sidle up next to them to show them something. Transition from the dinner table to the couch (love seat). Never sit in separate chairs after dinner. You want to be side by side, bodies touching, minds connecting.

TIMING OH SO SUBLIME

Timing is crucial in any successful endeavor. Nothing benefits or suffers from timing like the first move. You need to pounce when Jupiter has aligned with Pluto while Saturn's moon is rising—aka when the time is right. Read the signs like a blind man with Braille porn. Wait for that perfect moment before you bust a move and nut. Trust your gut. You will see it telegraphed through physicality and conversation. Wait for that window to open. Never let that rarified moment pass you by. And never try to pry open a shut window of op-porn-tunity. Don't halt a perfectly awesome night by ramming your tongue down their throat at the wrong time.

Wrong Times to Pounce

Their mouth is full

When they first arrive

They go in/come out of
bathroom

After belching loudly

When discussing tragedy

While they cry

After they mention the ex

Between bouts of food
poisoning

AWKWARD PAUSES

Oh, the awkward pause. Sigh. It's the stuff that dreams are made of. Awkward isn't always a bad thing. These are merely windows of opportunity for you to pounce. Never hesitate. Don't be bashful and bring up something trivial like it being perfect weather for seal-clubbing. Better yet, don't talk at all. A pregnant pause is a green light for you to approach with your mouth. Your date will either kiss back or give you their cheek. If it's the latter, remember: no shame and no regrets!

MAKING YOUR MOVE

This should be the natural progression if you read all the signs and observe the rules of the game suggested here. Go with the sexy flow and be triumphant. The vibe is either there or it's not. Bonus points for creativity. My greatest successes start when there's an awkward pause while I'm in close proximity. I squeeze their hand. If they squeeze back, it's on!

YOUR (FIRST) MOVE, SLICK

Back Rub
Few people will refuse a rub down.

Palm Reading

I see lots of banging in your future.

Compare Hand Sizes

The bigger the hand, the bigger the lust.

Waltz Around Your Pad

Dip them and kiss them.

Tell Them to Close Their Eyes

Then give them a sloppy wet surprise.

Ask If They'd Be Offended If You Kiss Them

Don't wait for a response.

Hand-feed Them

Follow it up with something equally delicious.

Place Food Between Your Teeth

Dare them to take a bite.

One for Stoners

Take a puff of weed and shotgun the smoke into their mouth.

RED LIGHT/GREEN LIGHT

So it's finally on. You Cooked to Bang like a champ and now you have your tongue in their mouth. Some dates can't wait for you to tear off their clothes like a barbarian. But some hookups can be skittish, like wounded deer. Don't scare them back into the brush by being too aggressive. By that same token, don't wimp out being too much of a gentleman or lady. You need to find the line between prude and whore.

Most dates decide how far they will go long before they show up. Your goal is to manipulate them into thinking it was their decision to bang you. Take your time building momentum. Unless this is a quickie, don't push too hard, too fast. Never underestimate the effectiveness of foreplay. Spend time stroking their hair and back, kissing their neck, nibbling their ears. Then grab their hips and ass, pulling them toward you. The object of these baby steps is to get them so hot and bothered they can't say no. Take this opportunity to see how far you can creep without coming off like a creep.

KITCHEN–BEDROOM TRANSITION PHRASES

Say	Never Say
Let's get something straight between us.	Clap your hands if you want the clap.
Your clothing has an appointment with my bedroom floor.	You could barely taste the roofies with all that basil.
Do you like traveling? Shangri La is in the next room.	You remind me of my ex.
The fashion police will have to confiscate those clothes.	Shh! We don't want to wake my parents.
Let's play hide-and-seek. I'll go first. (Hide under covers naked.)	I want my first time to be special.

Cook to Bang Golden Hookup Rules

- **Kiss:** Never lead with your tongue like the creature from Jabba's Pit of Sarlacc.
- **Spanking:** Their reaction is an indicator of how much fun they'll be.

- **Dry-humping:** Get them used to your thrusts for when the clothes melt off.
- **Dirty talk:** A personal choice that carries more risk than rewards, sugar tits.
- **Stay couch bound:** Don't suggest retiring to the bedroom. You'll get further on the love seat.
- **Migrating south:** Test uncharted waters with caution. Avoid crotch land mines.
- **Feeling up:** Graze first, then caress, before reaching under the bra for grand prize.

12

Advanced CTB: Culinarylingus

Ignore your mother's chiding to not play with your food. If you can't have a little fun with your nosh, you can sit in the corner and eat paste. Those with an adventurous palate read on. Bringing food into your fornicating makes something decadent delicious. It's a scrumptious twist on foreplay. My most memorable New Year's celebration was a homemade sushi party for two. We ate sushi off each other's naked bodies and used our navels like soy sauce dishes. It got us both so hot that we banged in every room in the house. Most memorable sushi dinner EVER!

Culinarylingus will help you discover what really turns them on as you lick them clean. Make this the most delicious banging session ever. Culinarylingus brings you two closer and gets you further in a hookup. You'll never think about food in the same way. We're talking memories you can recall when you're in a nursing home in soiled diapers and the only pleasure you get is from a plate of Jell-O and *Law and Order* reruns. Playing with your food opens your sexplorations to all manner of activities. Sensual, edible games are at your disposal depending on what you are playing with.

CULINARYLINGUS ACTIVITES

Edible Orgasm Indicators
Place food where you want extra attention.

Pimping Picasso
Turn their body into a culinary canvas you will ravage.

Blind Man Bluff
What are you tasting? Get it right, get a treat. Get it wrong . . .

Popsicle or Cocksicle?
Explanation unnecessary.

CULINARYLINGUS DOS AND DON'TS

Using someone's body as a plate is a delightful way to nourish yourself. But always exercise caution. A good idea like combining food and sex can become a bad idea like setting your own genitals on fire with hot sauce. There are foods that work to glorious effect and some that cock-block your efforts. Let common sense guide you to the right part of the market to buy your goods. Avoid anything that would be messy or painful. Aphrodisiacs are always par for the course with the uncomfortable exception of chiles. A word to the wise: always set a towel, newspaper, or plastic sheeting below to avoid stains you don't want to remember for years to come.

Do	Don't
Whipped cream	Sandwiches
Berries	Mayonnaise
Sashimi/sushi	Pizza
Chocolate	Salami
Ice cubes	Taco salad
Pineapple	Chili peppers
Popsicles	Hot sauce
Honey	

DOS

Whipped Cream

The culinarylingus canon classic. Whipped cream is a tad predictable, but there's a reason why it's the go-to lickable lubricant. No doubt, the 50s housewives made creamy dreamy whoopee with the mailman while the kids were at school. Whipped cream is sweet and suggestive of the final act of consummation. You can manipulate it in all sorts of fun ways. Spell out commands like *EAT ME, LICK HERE, YUM, I LOVE YOU*, etc. Form yourself a bikini or mankini. You could even snort a whip-it hit while you orgasm. Be careful not to overindulge because dairy lowers your libido.

Berries

Strawberries, blueberries, blackberries, boysenberries, acai berries, dingleberries. So many glorious choices. Devirginize yourself with a variety of sizes, colors, and flavors. Create a colorful collage across your date's chest and suck them up one by one. Bonus that they resemble the nipply nibbly bits. Raspberries and blackberries make great pasties. Berries won't fill you up and are bursting with juicy antioxidants to keep you in the game. Be aware that berry juice stains on Monica Lewinski's blue dress stained Bill Clinton's rep.

Sashimi/Sushi

Like I said, the best sushi dinner I ever ate was off a girl's tits. Wealthy Japanese businessmen pay small fortunes to eat off a naked woman. You are saving cash this way. High-quality raw fish delivers aphrodisiac payloads where it counts. The protein and sexy time flavor revs you both up and the texture is not unlike certain parts of a woman's anatomy. Suck and savor, my friends. Enjoy the cold fish on your warm skin. Just be sure to use only the freshest fish so no one gets sick by your sickening pursuit of sexual thrills.

Chocolate

Cocoa crack reporting for duty. Chocolate is the sweetest sexual stimulant around. There's no danger of passing out when you have chocolate-covered naughty bits. It forms and melts like a yummy clay that can be molded over and licked clean. Chocolate dances so elegantly back and forth between two mouths. It's like a relationship that changes and shrinks until it dissolves completely. Present your date with a box of chocolate, the gift that keeps on giving. But never let the chocolate slip too far down or it might be mistaken for a similarly colored substance . . . unless that's your thing.

Ice Cubes

Frozen H_2O is where the party's at! We're talking about the sex toy that melts and never stains. It's sugar-free frozen fun available in any freezer. You can freeze them into a pornocopia of shapes. Ice offers a rush of sensations to your pleasure receptors. Hot and cold on your most sensitive areas makes your toes curl. Tease your date by rubbing a cube up and down their body. Indulge in a snow job: cunninglingus or felatio performed with an ice cube in mouth. Now that's refreshing!

Pineapple

Desecrate SpongeBob SquarePants's home. What would the censors say? You couldn't care less considering how refreshing and delicious chunks of this yellow citric joy are. Replenish those calories you burnt banging. Pineapple pasties anyone? If that ain't enough, pineapple juice makes man juice tastes less spermy. Those pleasure-filled protein shakes will cause less gagging and more gargling. Just beware of SpongeBob's revenge: the spiky tops can blind you and the citric acid will burn eyes and other orifices.

Popsicles

It's hard to imagine anything more suggestive than the ice-cold phallic Popsicle. Like penises, they come in all sizes, shapes, and flavors. Guys, do yourself a favor and shop for Popsicles that match your stats. You don't want to be shown up by something frozen and fruity. Few things are more refreshing than a Popsicle before, after, or during steamy summer sex. I once used a Popsicle to seduce a girl at a music festival. She put the Popsicle way down her throat, inspiring me to bail on the show for the backseat of her Honda.

Honey

The birds and the bees. Question: what's so sexy about birds? It's all about the bees who make the sticky sweet nectar of the ancient gods. It's hard enough to keep your tongue out of the honey when it's on food. Try resisting some sticky icky on supple skin. Lick, lick, lick it clean. Be careful not to get the ancient aphrodisiac in your hair or on your clothes, sheets, or furniture. I overheard a raging slut coach her friend about giving head. She imagines herself as Winnie-the-Pooh licking a honey jar clean. I never experienced her mouth's herpes-go-round, but I do take the same lick-'em-clean-'til-they-scream approach.

DON'TS

Sandwiches

My love for sandwiches borders on obsession. But sandwiches don't belong in bed. The beauty of the sandwich is the endless combination of ingredients. That means endless possibilities for spillage. You don't want sandwich bits mixed up with naughty bits. Keep the sandwich in the fridge for a banging intermission snack. Settle for making a human sandwich where the bedsheets become slices of bread. Like the Detroit Grand Pubahs say:

You can be the bun
And I can be the burger, girl!

Mayonnaise

Weren't you paying attention to what I said about sandwiches? Mayonnaise is just not culinarylingus material. Enough people hate it on a sandwich let alone slathered over their body. It belongs on bread far away from your bedsheets. The only thing creamy that belongs in the bed rhymes with *hum*. And if you think mayonnaise would make a good lubricant, may I suggest huffing air freshener instead?

Pizza

I do love me some piping hot pizza loaded with all manner of ingredients like sausage and spicy jalapeños. Delicious? Yes. Sexy? No. The only thing steamy hot that belongs in your bed is your date's body. That body may not look as hot with third-degree burns. Pizza is best indulged in before or after intense calorie-burning banging sessions.

Salami

Aren't you planning on playing hide the salami later anyway? Why confuse things? First off, guys, you will be overshadowed unless you are packing some serious kielbasa. And most dates aren't down for object porn. Save your fetish for a kinky Eastern European who is into sausage play. Vegetarians make up a large portion of the dating population. Chances are they won't be turned on by meat by-products stuffed into intestines.

Taco Salad

The taco salad is the greatest culinary abomination known to man. Its existence makes holy men question their maker. There is nothing sexy about a salad fattier than a chili cheeseburger. Salads are supposed to be nutritious, not oozing with obesity. You'll go flaccid at the thought of getting down among the cream dressing, questionable meat, fart-powered beans, and sharp tortilla strips. Painful, messy, and piggy piggy.

Hot Sauce

Have you ever chopped up chili peppers and then rubbed your eyes or urinated? The burn is bloodcurdling. We're talking pain so extreme you'd opt for water-boarding. Spicy food and sensitive areas do not mix. I love spicy to the point of burning off my tongue with food, but not while banging. That doesn't mean skip spicy food at dinner, because that will help lead to a memorable evening. But remember that hot sauce is no substitute for lube.

13

S.O.S.:
Save Our Seduction

SHIT FALLS APART

There is no such thing as a sure thing. Murphy's law kicks you in the nuts whenever you get cocky. It may be humiliating, uncomfortable, or just plain awful. But you must see through your investment. An amateur kitchen Casanova might give up, but a Cook to Bang chef will work out a contingency plan and bang anyway. You may see it coming or get blindsided. I've had girls on my bed, legs spread, demanding a proper pounding when a friend calls from jail needing bail money. What do you do? (For the record: bang your date quickly, then rescue your homie.)

DON'T GIVE UP

You never want to lose the vibe or momentum when you're getting down. Don't let hookup hiccups discourage you. You invest a lot of time, money (for groceries), and energy into your end goal of banging. A savvy investor sees through their investment to profit. There are the occasional lost causes that seemed so promising, but then shiv you in the shower. But a clever reader like you will turn crisis into opportunity and reap the randy rewards. You deserve to win so go get what's yours.

FIGURE IT OUT

If your stylo ain't flying, adjust your strategy and approach. There is more than one route to any destination. If you can't get somewhere by car, go by air, sea, or dig a tunnel (these are metaphors, by the way). Be resourceful when you go after what you want. You'll find a way if it's worth it. Use logic, manipulation, and magic if you must to keep the banging vibe alive. You will end up with an embarrassment of riches. Or was that kisses?

FLATULENCE

Farts are a turnoff no matter how you stack them up. Air biscuits kill the vibe faster than you screaming, "Check out these cool genital warts!" But flatulence is natural. Even the hottest asses blow foul air. Only a hippie would find it cute or beautiful. The rest of us find it rancid and will gasp for fresh air.

Flatulence occurs when food does not get digested properly in your stomach and small intestine. When this undigested food reaches your large intestine, bacteria breaks it down and it ferments. It's the result of eating foods that aren't very nutritious or are so healthy they are cleansing all the nasty shit rotting in your guts. Ass gas can also be a result of a turd in the pipe that needs to be evacuated before you kill all plant life in the vicinity. Avoid fart-inducing foods before and during the date so you don't toot "Heartbreak Hotel" all alone.

FART WITH DISCRETION

Excuse Yourself
Let it rip outdoors or in the bathroom. Create noise like banging trash cans or running the sink to hide the sound of your toxic ass ripping a hole in the ozone layer. Turn on a fan or allow the gas trail to dissipate.

Ventilation
Position yourself near a fan, window, or air duct and let it rip.

Noise Buffer
Cover up the fart sounds with a sneeze or cough. There's not a whole lot you can do about the smell.

Fart Muffler
Think of a pillow or cushion like a silencer on a gun. The soft material will absorb the sound and some of the smell.

Crop Dusting

You can drain the pressure slowly walking around to spread out the offending air.

Burp It Out

The gassy pressure can be released out of your mouth. Be sure to drink something to disguise the belch stench.

Let It All Out

When you drop a NaGASaki bomb, make sure you get it all out. You don't want lingering soldiers in your trenches making a surprise attack later.

Blame Your Pet

Usually the dog. A cat, gerbil, or unicorn will also work.

If They Fart

Your call. Try to ignore and focus on how hot their ass looks rather than what's coming out of it. Try not to acknowledge it. They're already embarrassed. If it's loud enough to wake the neighbor's dog, laugh it off. Try rating the fart Olympics-style: 8.7!

Fart-Powered Foods	
Apricots	Brussels sprouts
Asparagus	Cabbage
Bananas	Carbonated drinks
Beans	Carrots
Bran	Cauliflower
Broccoli	Celery

Cheese	Nuts
Cucumbers	Popcorn
Dairy products	Prunes
Dried fruits	Raisins
Eggplant	Radishes
Fried foods	Rutabagas
Gravy	Sauerkraut
Ice cream	Tuna
Indian food	Turnips

CULINARY LIFE SUPPORT

Food doesn't always end up looking like the glamorized pictures in the cookbook. You may be unlucky or inept. Whatever the reason, you just blew the meal, the linchpin of your seduction. Don't panic! Accidents happen. Some food can be brought back from the great dinner plate in the sky. Don't give up on a dish, just like you don't give up on your Cook to Bang campaign because your ego got a booboo. Be the EMT that resuscitates the meal through gumption and resourcefulness.

Burnt to a Crisp

Scrape off as much of the burnt parts as possible. Disguise your blunder with herbs, spices, and sauces galore. Act like the dish is supposed to be charred.

Undercooked

If the food is undercooked, finish cooking it! Never risk trichinosis or salmonella with pork or chicken. Your date will be patient so long as the other courses are great and you charm their panties off.

Overcooked

You can save overcooked and dry food with moisture. Oil, butter, and sauces can do the trick. Drown that parched desert you call a meal so it doesn't give your date cottonmouth.

Food on the Floor

It all depends on how clean your floor is and how squeamish your date is. Let's hope they didn't witness your blunder. Swoop it up fast, apply the ten-second rule, and wash it off. Grosser things have happened.

Overspiced Food

Food can be rendered inedible by too much flavor. Douse the offending sauce, veggies, meat, etc., with water and then drain the excess liquid. You'll lose some texture, but you will also remove much of the offending flavor. Or make more of whatever you are serving and let the flavor spread out.

Watery Food

Sauces can turn out watery or runny when they are supposed to be thick. Thicken the consistency by reducing it over low heat or add flour, cornstarch, tomato paste, or pectin. Add a little at a time so your meal doesn't become a hardened mess.

Thick Food

If your meal looks like the tar pit the last T. rex was swallowed up in, create more room by adding some water or stock (vegetable, chicken, beef, etc.). Stir in a little at a time until you re-create the perfect consistency.

Stinky Food

Your culinary masterpiece might smell off or just plain nasty. Disguise that smell so your dish has its day in court. Try spices and herbs with overpowering scents like lavender, rosemary, fresh basil, cilantro, nutmeg, or cinnamon.

SPILLS AND THRILLS

I'm a total klutz who has been thrown out of many a party for breaking valuables. It harkens back to my childhood in the 80s when I dropped my yellow Sony Walkman while listening to Weird Al's "Eat It." I am also a master of spilling food, drink, and lube all over expensive furniture, rugs, and even the ceiling. These spills ruin not only valuables, but also your banging momentum.

I've adapted to my many flaws and react fast to turn follies into jollies. It's important to know the correct course of action so you can quickly return to naked party time. The number one rule of spill recovery is to dab at the mess. Don't rub it into the precious surface. A wise Cook to Banger will be prepared with paper towels, rags, a sponge, club soda, and carpet cleaner handy at all times. If your date spills, it will be easier to make your move. They owe you one.

Clothing Spills

If you spill on your own clothes in your own pad, no big deal. You can change or perform a strip tease. But you need a contingency plan if your date's clothes are tainted. Chances are they like the outfit since they wore it on a date. Apologize, ease the tension with humor, and handle the crisis with a smile. Hopefully you at least have a washer/dryer in your building. Confiscate the ruined garment, use a stain remover, and wash it. This just bought you a good extra hour with your now half-naked date. Get undressed if that makes them feel more comfortable. Or loan them one of your shirts temporarily. You'll come off like the keeper you are.

At least now they'll have clean clothes tomorrow for their walk of shame.

Carpet Spill

Clothing is expendable when you trash it. Like a diamond, carpet stains are forever. You better be quick on your feet if you want to maintain a stain-free existence. Should food fall, push your buck-naked date off you so you can pick it off the carpet and start cleaning. Dab up all moisture until it's bone dry. Now bust out a fresh bottle of club soda. The flat bottle that's been in your fridge since you made vodka sodas six months ago won't cut it. Pour the fresh bubbly over the spill in small amounts and dab away. Just like cunnilingus, work it repeatedly until you get results. Finally, bust out the carpet cleaner and let it set in before scrubbing. Back to naughty naked time!

Furniture Spill

Are you that clumsy that you spill on the goddamn furniture? There's something seriously wrong with you. Best of luck forgiving yourself. This cleanup process is similar to the carpet, but requires a more ginger touch. The difference is that you can move furniture around to hide a carpet stain, but there are stains no throw pillow can disguise. Your future conquests are in danger, especially if the stain is chocolate brown. A stained couch is the scarlet letter of immaturity. You don't want your date thinking you still live in a frat house. Be fast, methodical, and get back to the task at hand.

Red Wine Spill

Nothing stains like red wine (besides blood; vampires, you are on notice). You must respond with the reflexes of a jungle cat. The solution lies in red wine's nemesis: white wine! First dab up as much of the red as possible, then cover the stain with white wine. Allow the white wine acids to eat away at the red wine tannins before dabbing it all up. Repeat the process until you remove as much red as possible. Follow it up with club soda and carpet cleaner if needed.

SPIT TRICK

When you have no white wine or club soda, use saliva. The enzymes in your spit will eat away at the tannins. Make it a game. Get your date to help you spit on the stain and then make your move.

Broken Glass

Clean that shit up, stat! I wager neither of you wants to bleed to death while in the throes of lust. You want the possibility of banging on the floor without the threat of shredding your genitals. First clear the area. Be the hero and carry your date out of the danger zone. Fetch close-toed shoes and get to work. First pick up the shards big and small off the ground. Now vacuum up the remaining pieces. A dustpan and broom are a decent alternative, but you risk overlooking shards invisible to the eye that will hurt your bare feet.

DATE CATCHES ON FIRE

Your prospects for banging decrease when you set your date on fire. Was it really necessary to demonstrate your ability to juggle fire indoors after three glasses of wine? It's like spilling wine

on their best white shirt, but requires much faster reflexes and a sincere apology. Be sure to put out the flames by any means necessary. Burn victims are not sexy. Use any liquid available like water, (cold) soup, or wine, but avoid hard liquor unless you want to see fireballs. Smother them with a blanket. Hose them down with pee if you must. Make sure the fire is contained. Douse any embers, smoke, or ash. You don't want to burn down your place or the whole neighborhood. Your neighbors will likely sue you, even if you Cook to Bang every last one of them.

UNEXPECTED GUEST

Some people have the worst timing. There you are on the verge of closing the deal, Barry White's soothing hot chocolate voice echoes in your head. Your night is sure to be bang-a-licious—when cock-blocking takes effect. It may be your roommate or a friend wondering if you TiVo'ed *Lost*, or worst of all, your ex. You hope they realize their trespass and fuck off. But some people are so daft or vindictive they won't leave.

I was on the verge of a threesome in college at a party with both girls on the bed getting familiar with each other. My girlfriend was kissing her friend's neck while I rubbed

their shoulders with lotion. It was like a porno starring me.
But then three of my drunk buddies just back from a Wide-
spread Panic concert burst in to tell me all about it. My idiotic amigos cock-blocked this hall of fame moment. They
kept talking and talking; I should have been banging and
banging. I had to listen to the minute details of a concert I
skipped for a reason while my porno costars walked right
out the door.

HOW TO GET RID OF UNEXPECTED GUESTS

Don't Answer the Door

Ignore them and they might go away. If your date asks why, say
it's your drunk neighbor at the wrong door again. You aren't
expecting anyone anyway, which is true.

Pull the Intruder Aside

Explain the obvious using the visual aid of your half-naked
date. Hopefully they aren't too daft or indifferent to understand and leave. Only a true fuck-nut will stick around once
they realize they are cock-blocking your shit.

Bribe Them

Give them whatever they came for. No matter the cost, you'll
be glad to hand it over and send them on their way. You can
always offer them five dollars to spend at the arcade far away
from you.

Move into the Bedroom

Make up an excuse to go somewhere more private. You could
show them a photo album or a piece of art. The interruption

makes the move to your banging quarters seem innocent, which works to your advantage.

Chase Them Out with a Baseball Bat

Sometimes the threat of violence is the only antidote for stupidity. They will get off your property in a hurry. Don't actually hit them unless you like cops and lawsuits. In that case, tell the judge it was all in the name of banging.

YOU OFFEND THEM

I sometimes manage to blow dates that seemed like slam dunks. My big, offensive mouth gets in the way. I was hooking up with a girl who was teasing me all night. So when her hair got messed up after an intense game of tonsil hockey, I said, "You look like a bag lady." Her fuck-me-now eyes turned into an I-will-eat-your-soul glare. "I mean a really hot bag lady!" wasn't enough to keep her from storming off. That's why it's important to avoid controversial topics. You never know what might get some prude's panties in a bunch.

CONVINCE THEM TO STAY

Pretend It Was a Joke
Spin it, claiming you were testing to see how they would react.

Just a Misunderstanding
You were talking about two entirely different things.

They Misheard You
Clarify your statement with something innocent.

You're a Bad Boy/Girl

It's human nature to want to be treated like a toilet.

Beg Them to Stay

Show remorse. You earn yourself some bang-free cuddling.

THE EX CALLS

Regardless of whose ex calls, if the call is taken, your game is FUBAR! Emotional psycho-babble chased with blue balls, yum! Even if the date was going swimmingly, a seed of doubt has been planted in a broken heart. Do yourself a favor and never take your ex's call on a date. It's already a bad sign if your date is playing with their phone. Best of luck if they take that call. Should they miraculously not run out the door in tears or to their ex's for makeup sex, you better ramp the vibe back up, stat.

I once Cooked to Bang for a recent divorcée as an experiment in NSA (no strings attached) sexploitation. She was impressed that I cooked for her since her lousy ex-husband didn't even make her eggs during their sham marriage. But she took the brute's call, cried on my porch, and then excused herself. I saw on Facebook later that they had gotten back together. Glad to be of service . . . to everyone but myself.

REVIVE THE VIBE

Don't Address the Call

Just play it off like nothing happened.

Offer No Judgment
Be all smiles all the time.

Change the Subject
Return to an earlier topic that made them laugh and smile.

Ease Back into It
Don't rush it. You will have plenty of time for rebound sex.

Top Off Their Glass
A little sippy sip never hurts when you're feeling blue.

Play That Funky Music
Turn the pity party into a dance party.

Forget about Those Woes
Wiggle your toes!

OVERUSING THE BOOZE

Boozing can be fun and sexy. But awesome it is not to have someone puking in the kitchen sink. This trashy cry for help has no place on a Cook to Bang date. Getting tipsy and brazen is one thing, because it leads to nudity. But when you lose control, you lose the game. Should all standards get yakked down the drain, make sure you are both consensually trashed. Date rape is illegal, amoral, and pathetic. The Cook to Bang method is strong enough to be pulled off sober. Right that boozy ship without drowning the vibe.

SOBER THAT ASS UP!

Fresh Air Does a Drunk Good
Make sure Hotty McDrunkle gulps a ton of oxygen.

Drink Up, Fool
Flush the booze and rehydrate with nonalcoholic fluids.

Rev 'Em Back Up
Caffeinated drinks like coffee, tea, and soda can reset the game.

Exercise the Demons
If you can't bang, take a walk, run, or roll down a hill.

Stretch It Out
Work out the kinks in the cloudy brain with a private yoga session.

NO CHEMISTRY

Best of luck with this dilemma. You might be able to kick-start the attraction just by being awesome. A fresh approach might warm over their icy heart. But sometimes one of you just won't be feeling it. If this date is the hottest piece of ass you'll ever lure into your sex lair, only drastic measures will do. Snatch victory out of the jaws of defeat. Here are methods to combat the following:

Boring or Annoying Date

REMEMBER IT'S ABOUT BANGING: You didn't invite them over for their personality.

TAKE CONTROL OF THE CONVERSATION: Discuss subjects that aren't dull as shit.

PUSH THEIR BUTTONS: Ask ridiculous questions to amuse yourself.

BANG THEM WITH THEIR FACE DOWN IN THE PILLOW: They can't get on your nerves that way.

No Sense of Humor

CHANGE UP YOUR JOKES: Not everyone thinks you are as funny as you do.

STOP BEING A CLOWN: Some people just don't like to laugh, but love to bang.

DON'T OFFEND THEM: The slut in pastel might go back into their conservative shell.

STOP TRYING SO HARD: Just be yourself and let that be enough.

No Sexual Chemistry

START DRINKING MORE: Dust off the martini shaker and lower your standards.

BE CHILDISH: Play Truth or Dare or Never Have I Ever and see where it leads.

START A DANCE PARTY: Get them grooving to music they like and rub up on them.

JUST MAKE YOUR MOVE: They will either bang you or leave. Win win!

THEY WON'T LEAVE AFTER

Ever find yourself lying postcoital next to a lesser alternative to a dead hobo? They may be another notch on your bedpost, revenge fuck, or you were just bored. Take evasive action to get them out of your bed and life or you'll be in for the long haul. You're fucked once they throw their leg over yours, lock you into an inescapable bear trap, snuggle, and snore loud enough to wake your neighbor's deaf labrador. You contemplate hari-kari when they want to DTR (Discuss the Relationship), where you don't see a future past the bye-bye blowjob. It's not pretty come morning light when the alcohol has run its course. Find a way to convince them to take their shit and leave without upsetting the herd. Here's how to shake them loose so you can get your beauty rest . . . alone.

Early Morning Conference Call

Cliché but useful. Feign disappointment. Insist that you need to get some sleep due to the importance of the call. Ramble on about technical work details, and then trail off. They will be bored and take the hint.

"Your Car Will Get Towed!"

Every car owner has built-in paranoia about their car when they are parked away from home. Getting a ticket or towed is a rub that might dissuade them from lingering, but not always. Just inform them their car will be impounded if they spend the night.

Fake an Emergency

It all starts with a phone call, preferably from an alarm set on your phone. You take the call, react like a Broadway actor, and assure the imaginary caller you will be there soon. My favorite reason is bailing a friend out of jail for a DUI. But any 911 will do.

Pray for Nuclear Holocaust

If all else fails, you can always indulge in your world annihilation fantasy. Chances are this will be a step up from having that annoying lump of shit snoring next to you. At least it will be quick and painless, unless you survive then prepare for the . . .

ZOMBIE UPRISING

Your nuclear holocaust fantasy came true. Now it's just you and your date with whom you'd gladly share this brave new world with. It will be up to you to repopulate the earth eventually. Cook to Bang will become a whole lot more important when every waiter and cook becomes a brain-hungry zombie. Remember, if you can't pierce the living deads' skulls, you are lunch. No banging.

14

Cook to Bang
Testes-moan-ials

Cooktobang.com began as a hobby to keep me busy between writing gigs. But the love letters e-mailed to me by folks who successfully Cook to Bang'ed told me I was onto something. Strangers' triumphs with my recipes and methods inspire me to continue to spread the Cook to Bang gospel. Some would say I am doing God's work. I agree. I was once a pathetic shell of a man struggling to get laid and failing epically. Now I pull more ass than a Burger King toilet seat. Below are some of my favorite love letters from Cook to Bang enthusiasts.

PETER IN NEW YORK

Just wanted to let you know, I finally tried out your recipes last night. I made the Forbidden Fruit Salad as an appetizer, followed it up with the Friction Chicken Salad, blew her mind with the MISO HORNY COD, and finished with the Pinch-Your-Ass-Berry Brownies à la mode. Everything turned out AWESOME. I followed all of your recipes to the letter and the food was amazing. My girlfriend was so impressed she told her parents about it!

JAY IN CHICAGO

I'm an insensitive douche bag that drove his supportive girl-friend away. So I wanted to show her I'm not always shallow and narcissistic. A friend suggested cooking her a heartfelt meal so I Googled seduction recipes and happened upon the Oysters Rockafella Skank. I surprised her when she got home from work with a badass meal. She loved the food almost as much as she loved hearing "I love you." Now I'm debating which CTB dish to make when I pop the question.

GARY IN LOUISVILLE

I talked my curvy neighbor into stopping by to watch a Satur-day afternoon game, playing it off as casual. When she showed up in jeans and a ball cap with a bag of chips and a six-pack I offered to whip up something more substantial. I came out of the kitchen fifteen minutes later with Pesto Bango! Chicken Sinwiches. She was blown away. By halftime, I was blown, too. All that grease on our fingers came in handy. The shit is workin'.

MADELINE IN LOS ANGELES

I felt inclined to comment on how Cook to Bang helped a girl out. I am in a relationship with a great guy, but I never knew how to get some serious morning action. Thanks to Sex Crazy Mofo Tofu Scramble, my boyfriend went all sex crazy after breakfast. I didn't have a lot to complain about before, but I am endlessly happy with the sweet morning loving I am getting now. Thanks so much for your savory suggestions. Cook to Bang works for girls, too.

ANDREW IN CHARLOTTE

My game was so bad my friends thought I was gay. Girls always thought of me as their guy friend that they could say anything to except for "I want to ride you like a pony." Thanks to the Cook to Bang tips and the Baked Briez Nuts recipe, I felt like Seabiscuit after eight furlongs. The perfect breakthrough for the "Let's just be friends" talk.

BRETT IN SAN FRANSISSY

Adaptable to any orientation it seems, CTB is a gay man's culinary paradise. Even if he's deeply buried in the closet, his stone wall will come crashing down once his buds get a taste. And if you manage to save room for dessert, finish him off with the creamy and infinitely swallowable Stroke My Bananas Foster. Thanks, CTB, for showing a "girl" a good time and helping "her" to get that man geared up and firing on all cylinders.

MATT IN MILWAUKEE

Thank God for this site! I live down the hall from this Australian girl and finally grew the balls to ask her out. Because of your brilliant theory I invited her over for dinner. I don't know if the pear and avocado were aphrodisiacs or if it was the wine or the fact that the bedroom was just a few feet away, but it was the easiest time I'd ever had visiting down under. Thanks for the recipes. Keep 'em coming! I've got to keep this up!

RANDALL IN COLORADO SPRINGS

My girlfriend of five years' strict upbringing has left her somewhat reluctant and unadventurous in the bedroom. That was until I introduced her to Raging Hard (On) Lemonade. She never cared much for the flavor of alcoholic drinks but she loves the taste of this libido juice and it turns her on like a fire hose. Now she's my precious loving slut. Lately, just the sound of the blender brings a frisky smile to her face. Tonight, I'm adding Tap That Ass-paragus Soup to the mix and she's promised to include a few new menu items of her own.

MICHAEL IN PORKLAND

Up here in Oregon there's little tail that hasn't expired or gone lumberjill. But when you do find one you can't just be another emo hipster with a cool tattoo. Cook to fucking Bang! That's why they call it wining and *dining* them. That In-slut-ada Caprese Salad cost me a short trip to Trader Joe's and a three-pack of Magnums.

STEPHEN IN VANCOUGAR

My coworker, Miss Snotty Hot Blonde who gave me absolutely zero coffee room play, was forced by circumstance to drop off some office crap at my place one evening. She showed up at the door ready to drop and bolt, but, as luck would have it, I had a batch of Pinch-Your-Ass-Berry Brownies in the oven and the smell stuck to two fingers up her nose and pulled her in like a balloon on a string. She wolfed down the results and practically begged for seconds. We finished off the brownies together before she finished me off. You're my hero!

MAC IN SPLITSVILLE

My skank-hole ex did all the cookin' when we were together. But ever since the cheating skeeze-bag ran off with her new boyfriend I needed to learn to do it myself. Thanks, Cook to Bang, for making my life way more delicious—in more ways the one.

AFTERWORD

Wrapping This
Shit Up ... Tight!

If you made it this far through the book without throwing it at the Jehovah's Witness that won't get off your porch, nice work! I hope this was half as enjoyable to read as it was to write. Writing about food and sex, food = sex, and sex with food has left me with a cerebral chubby. Thanks for taking this filthy ride with me from the market to the kitchen to the living room and finally ending up in bed with me. Warning: many girls have told me I snore.

My hope is, at the very least, that you are inspired to cook. I love cooking nearly as much as I love banging. When I'm feeling down or want to celebrate, the kitchen is where you'll find me. Cooking completes me. It's a game you play over a lifetime. You will perfect recipes the way you perfect your oral technique (hint: take your time). Cooking meals for yourself and others, dates or otherwise, will enrich your life. Worst-case scenario: your body and bank account will be in better shape. Please enjoy the shit out of my recipes and tricks and feel free to take credit for them with your dates. They are user-friendly and field-tested.

All tomfoolery aside, I believe wholeheartedly in the Cook

to Bang method. It will serve you well as it has hooked this average dude up rather nicely. Remember, I'm not that tall, handsome, or rich. But I pull out-of-my-league ass with confidence in myself and my food. Nothing should stop you from doing the same.

Cook, Bang, and prosper, my friends!

ACKNOWLEDGMENTS

First, I want to thank the women of the world. For those I have banged and those I plan on banging, thank you for motivating me. Whether I'm cooking, banging, writing, or writing about cooking and banging, it's all for you and you and especially YOU!

A big shout-out is due to my main man and editor, Yaniv Soha, at St. Martin's Press. This sexy bastard saw the raw potential of *Cook to Bang* and made this wet dream of mine possible. A better editor for a first-time author there could not be. Ladies, you are on notice.

Much props go out to my career wingmen. My managers, Rachel Miller and Jesse Hara of Tom Sawyer Entertainment, saw potential in *Cook to Bang* when it was a shitty, neglected Web site that got five unique visitors on a good day. They continue to help me shape *Cook to Bang* into a juggernaut that will become a household brand name like Trojan condoms or Bell Biv DeVoe.

My book agent, Jud Laghi, is also guilty of perpetrating this literary offense on the world. Jud knew he could sell *Cook to Bang*, and voila! Book deal. I'm glad this book-selling maestro is in my corner.

Super-lawyer Melissa Manfro deserves a massive muffin-basket line with gold bouillon for all her due diligence. I hope to someday wheelbarrow piles of $100 bills into your office for all your lawyerly support, not to mention friendship.

Cheers to all the folks I worked with over the years as a television writer, executive, assistant, coffee-bitch, and glorified Blockbuster employee. Those of you who believed in me, promoted me, fired me, or hurled staplers at my head all made me the unique snowflake I am today.

Lastly, I want to thank my family for putting up with my crap over the years. I know I wasn't the easiest kid to raise. Sorry my first book isn't some erudite and highfalutin literary opus that will be taught in Ivy League institutions for centuries to come. But you never know!